Edited and with an Introduction by

John Kenneth Galbraith

Recollections of the

N E W

D E A L

When the People Mattered

Thomas H. Eliot

Northeastern University Press / Boston

Northeastern University Press

The frontispiece photograph is by Martin Munkácsi, New York.

Library of Congress Cataloging in Publication Data
Eliot, Thomas Hopkinson, 1907–
Recollections of the New Deal : when the people mattered / Thomas
H. Eliot ; edited and with an introduction by John Kenneth
Galbraith.
p. cm.
Includes index.
ISBN 1-55553-134-2 (acid-free paper)
1. New Deal, 1933–1939. 2. United States—History—1933–1945.
3. Social security—United States—History. 4. Eliot, Thomas
Hopkinson, 1907– . I. Galbraith, John Kenneth, 1908– .
II. Title.
E806.E54   1992
973.917—dc20   92–18496

Designed by David Ford

Composed in Baskerville
by Graphic Composition, Inc., Athens, Georgia.
Printed and bound by
Princeton University Press, Lawrenceville, New Jersey.
The paper is Glatfelter Offset, an acid-free sheet.

MANUFACTURED IN THE UNITED STATES OF AMERICA
97 96 95 94 93 92 5 4 3 2 1

973.917
E

Contents

Illustrations

Thomas H. Eliot   *Frontispiece*

Appearing between pages 72 and 73

Hugh Johnson

Frances Perkins

Robert F. Wagner

John G. Winant

Roosevelt signing the Social Security Act

Frances Perkins and F.D.R.

Introduction

For a long time now the Institute of Politics of the Kennedy School of Government at Harvard has, every two years, invited the newly elected congressmen and congresswomen to Cambridge for a series of lectures and seminars on their new life on Capitol Hill and the issues with which they will contend. The program has traditionally included a late afternoon stopover at our house for a relaxed discussion of matters present and past.

For these gatherings my wife and I always invited Thomas Eliot to be present and to speak. It is not too much to say that the evening was his.

He told the new legislators about Washington in the days of the New Deal and in particular of the origin, preparation, and passage of the Social Security Act fifty and now more years back. It taxed their credulity: these men and women, so young by Eliot's (and my) standards, could scarcely believe that anyone was still alive who could speak so lucidly and so intimately of the birth of this truly historic legislation. I was occasionally disposed to wonder if someone would ask, had he not been present for the signing of the Emancipation Proclamation? Appearing, as not infrequently I do, before congressional committees, I have regularly been told of how well these sessions are remembered.

To be the principal author of the Social Security Act would sufficiently distinguish almost anyone and serve as the founding rock of a full career. For Eliot, known to all as Tom, there was a great deal more. He was the scion of a distinguished, in fact famous, New England family—his father, Samuel Atkins

Eliot, was a noted clergyman; his grandfather, Charles William Eliot, the most noted of Harvard presidents. With an undergraduate and law degree from Harvard, Tom Eliot went briefly into law practice and then to Washington in the early and luminous days of the New Deal, here so admirably described and on which I offer a later word. Then from writing legislation he went on to offering and passing it; he was elected to Congress in 1940 from the Ninth Massachusetts District. He was a well-respected congressman, but the Eliot term in office was brought to a close by redistricting and a consequent collision with the famous, many would say infamous, James Michael Curley. Taking note of his opponent's liberal reputation and voting record in Washington, Curley ran on the slogan "Curley or Communism." For many of Tom's constituents there was an undoubted uncertainty as to just what Communism might be, but if Jim Curley said it was bad, and notably a present threat to all good Catholics, so it was.

In later years Tom served in various Washington and overseas wartime posts, joined a distinguished Boston law firm which still bears his name, and then turned his attention seriously to academic work.

At Washington University in St. Louis he rose steadily through the academic ranks from professor to chancellor. He is remembered there as one of the most effective and resourceful occupants of the latter post, diligent in administration, determined in protection of academic expression, successful in money-raising, and supremely adept in dealing with the student and faculty dissension of the Vietnam years. Then, not retiring, he became, in 1971, the president of the Salzburg Seminar in American Studies, dividing his time between Austria and Cambridge. Always he had the intelligent, alert, and never-failing companionship and support of his wife, Lois Jameson Eliot, a presence in these pages.

Tom Eliot died of cancer in the autumn of 1991, almost on the day this book was completed. To Lois fell part of the task of assembling the manuscript for the publisher. I am denoted as editor. Perhaps were Tom alive, I would have argued with him on a point or two of prose style—he tells in the early pages of resisting a minor suggestion of mine as to metaphor, which he wholeheartedly rejected. But this is his book and so I have sought to have it remain. Nor, given his clear, exact, and warmly personal expression, will anyone regret that I did.

This is, in its way, two books. At the beginning and at the end it evokes the wonder of Washington in the F.D.R. and New Deal days. I was briefly employed in the Agricultural Adjustment Administration in 1934, and in the ensuing years, as were numerous Harvard economists, I was much in Washington on one assignment or another. While in the 1930s far less intimately a part of the scene than Eliot and with vastly less responsibility, I still have the sense of having been present at the creation, being there on "that dawn to be alive" of which Eliot here tells. And I do not exaggerate: nothing in the vast literature of F.D.R. and the New Deal better recaptures my sense of excitement than the pages that follow.

One is tempted to stress a point that the author by no means neglects. All or nearly all involved in this moment of American history were, by modern standards, incredibly young. So it continued during the war years. (In 1941, at the age of 33, if I may be allowed another personal note, I was placed in charge of all the prices in the United States—the wartime price czar. I have trouble imagining that I would now entrust such authority and responsibility to one so young.)

The reason for this explosive role of youth was partly economic. Older scholars, older lawyers, even older public servants were settled in employment, income, family, and position. They were not easily detached therefrom even by the Depression. The young, on the other hand, were wonderfully available. No other opportunity so beckoned, maybe even existed. And in the Depression years, the pay in Washington varied for the young from adequate to incredible. From a salary of $1,800 a year teaching at the University of California, I went, in 1934, to $3,200 in Washington. In a few months I had paid off all my college debts. Tom Eliot was an exceptional case: on going to Washington, he took a very modest cut in pay.

But there was something more, and more important. It was the challenge of the Depression itself that brought the young men and just a few women to Washington. With the problems then presented, an older generation could not or would not contend. Depressions were seen to be self-correcting; that was the nature of the business cycle. Error was with those who interfered with something assumed to be very closely akin to the normal processes of nature. So mainly it was the young who combined impatience with release from economic, political, and social orthodoxy and believed that something could be done. Because they so believed, there was a wondrous excitement.

As is here told, life in those days was a kind of perpetual seminar on economic and political action. One dealt with one's designated and specific responsibilities during the day, met with others for more extended and diverse discussion in the evening and well into the night. Tom Eliot, as these pages will leave no one in doubt, was at the very center. The country was in a condition of deep despair; people were truly suffering. Those so felicitously present bore, as they saw it, the grave responsibility for remedy and relief.

Perhaps for a brief time under John F. Kennedy there was a similar sense of privileged and highly responsible involvement. There has certainly not been since. It has been a long way down to the assertion of these last years that government is not the solution but the problem; that its welfare efforts are an inert burden; that its bureaucrats, those in the Pentagon apart, are a stodgy and incompetent affliction. No one reading the pages to come can fail to see the difference.

The second and, some will think, the historically more solid part of this book is the account, the firsthand account, of labor relations and the preparation for, and passage of, the Social Security Act. They may be right; here is history as it was being made.

The author in an intense chapter reminds us that the 1930s were, by any previous or subsequent standard, years of angry labor disputes. The NRA and further labor legislation legitimatized the labor union and collective bargaining. And they gave position and voice to a remarkable group of labor leaders. They did not, however, legitimatize unions in the eyes and minds of employers. With rare exceptions, the latter still thought the workers should be kept in their proper and non-assertive role. Their encouragement was another aberration of Roosevelt and the New Deal: it was the employers' task to resist and correct. From this came the inevitable and bitter conflict.

Into this caldron the young Eliot was plunged. Of the experience, with remarkable memory supported by diary and letters, he tells. His mediating role extended to the great waterfront confrontation and general strike in San Francisco, along with the Detroit sit-ins one of the two polar disputes of the decade. We will not again hear firsthand of this strike, which ended in the years-long effort to return Harry Bridges, as an alleged or perhaps more precisely an honorary Communist, to his native Australia, where he was ardently thought to belong.

The chapter on labor and strike mediation has a slightly disconnected quality. It tells of being here and there, in one dispute and the next. This is the way a mediator works. There is no similar problem in the next chapters. The origin, development, and passage of the Social Security legislation is told sequentially from beginning to end. One reason is that the author was there taking the major role from the beginning to the end.

One wonders if even today we fully appreciate the power of this legislation. In the last century and early in the present one capitalism had a cruel and ugly face. And the alienation and adverse action so stimulated were extreme. Along with the many who thought that the system should not survive were perhaps more who thought it could not survive. The European countries—Germany with Bismarck the pioneer, Britain under Lloyd George, France with more diffuse authority—had taken steps to mitigate the cruelties of old age, illness, and unemployment without income. Not so the United States.

Those who are most in need of economic salvation are often those who most resist it. The Social Security Act of 1935 was bitterly attacked by businessmen and by their spokesmen in Washington. The National Association of Manufacturers said that it would facilitate the "ultimate socialistic control of life and industry." John Taber, a highly articulate congressman from upstate New York, said, "Never in the history of the world has any measure been brought in here so insidiously designed . . . to enslave workers." His colleague Congressman Daniel Reed said, "The lash of the dictator will be felt." Yet the consequence in the longer run is not in doubt. This calming and ameliorative legislation took the worst and harshest edge off capitalism. With other action the system became more than tolerable and by earlier standards internally tranquil. That is what the Eastern Europeans and the people of the former Soviet Union saw when in the great revolution of 1989–91 they discarded Communism for the perilous path to the market economy.

The mellowing role of Social Security as regards economic hardship is now, of course, widely accepted. And its hold on public (and voter) opinion is, perhaps needless to say, not in doubt. I mentioned earlier that in the Reagan-Bush years those serving in the military and in the Pentagon were exempt from the harsh words that public servants generally were made to suffer. Exempt also in a quiet way were the anonymous figures who administered the old age pension system and unemployment compensation. A politician running for office in opposition to Social Security would be widely thought both politically and mentally defective. And this the polls would soon affirm. Tom Eliot authored and helped guide the passage of what is today perhaps the single most popular piece of legislation on the federal statute books.

It is not perfect; in every congressional session there is debate and often action over some measure to strengthen, extend, or improve it. The coverage and duration of unemployment compensation is now very much subject to discussion, as is also, if less intensely, the taxation of affluent old-age pensioners. Those who follow the debate or are affected by it are the natural audience for this book. So, I would like to think, are those for whom Social Security is the basic and frequently comfortable alternative to want and destitution. Here is how it all began; let all who now benefit have knowledge of that beginning. Of this the following pages tell as never quite before.

JOHN KENNETH GALBRAITH

Recollections of the New Deal

When the People Mattered

Chapter 1

Work and Play

 WHEN I asked a kindly book-
seller the other day for *Dealers and Dreamers,* a book about the
New Deal, he didn't have it. "The New Deal," he said with a
smile, "is old hat." He was reckoning not with the world to
come. The Roaring Twenties were followed by the Great
Depression. The Me-first Eighties will be followed by—what?

We have had recessions before and we will have them again;
and always, when we do, we can be thankful to the New Deal.
For nearly half a century, its innovations in the thirties have
helped to keep recession from deepening into depression. And
when and if there is a real crash, we will need to renew our
knowledge of how the New Deal dealt with the earlier one. Its
outlook and its spirit will be desperately needed if our economic skies really darken. Old hat, indeed!

Today if you read the history books you can absorb, unemo-
tionally, facts and figures describing the country's condition
sixty years ago: over twenty-five percent, thirty-three percent
in some cities, of the normal work force unemployed; bank
failures and bankruptcies up; local resources for "poor relief"
dwindling to the vanishing point. It takes a good deal of imagination to get stirred up by these gloomy old statistics. To
awaken your imagination you might try reading the two best-
selling novels of the Depression, Robert Nathan's *One More
Spring* and John Steinbeck's *The Grapes of Wrath.*

Still, the era may seem irrelevant. You will find it hard to
identify with Nathan's unemployed musician or destitute
banker, not to mention his warmhearted prostitute, and unless
you are acutely aware of today's homeless you'll have trouble

envisaging them living in a toolshed in Central Park. As for Steinbeck's plucky, desperate, drought-stricken farmers, you'll sympathize with their plight but you're sure that you yourself will never be an Okie.

How, then, can we make ourselves aware of the present relevance of the New Deal, and especially of what we owe it? Perhaps a comparison of what happened under certain circumstances to an individual just as Franklin D. Roosevelt was beginning his first term with what happens to that person now will do the trick. Consider:

In the early thirties you deposited your savings in a bank, the bank failed, and you lost all your money. In the nineties you deposit your savings in a bank (or, God save the mark, an S. & L.), it fails, and you get your money back.

Then, you needed a job and in 1935, say, you got one in a shoe factory, at a piece-work wage amounting to 80 cents. Today, in a comparable job, you can't legally be paid less than $4.50 an hour. Not too different, you think, considering inflation—but wait a minute! That wage that was perfectly legal in 1935 was not 80 cents an hour: it was 80 cents for an eight-hour *day.*

Then, at least until 1935, your employer could warn you that if you joined a labor union you would be fired; you joined one and indeed you were fired. Today you and your fellow employees have a right to join or even organize a union, and you can't be fired for doing so.

Then, if you lost whatever job you had and couldn't quickly find another, you might well have had nothing—literally nothing—to live on; your plight became the subject of that haunting song of the thirties, "Brother, Can You Spare a Dime?" Today, for many months while you seek employment, you have a small but steady income provided by your state's unemployment compensation system.

Then, when you were old and gray and full of years, if you had lost your savings in that defunct bank or in the virtually unregulated stock market, you'd need help and you'd get it, under your state old age pension law—help to the extent of $26 a month if you were lucky and lived in the most generous state, Massachusetts, but just $1.22 if you lived in Nebraska, or 69 cents—yes, 69 *cents*—if you lived in North Dakota. Today, each month you'll receive a federal social security check (average amount $600 plus) that will enable you at the very least to buy the groceries.

These differences between then and now are all due to what our government did then. And it could not have happened without there having been a further great difference. Often derided now, public service was welcomed and respected then.* The chance to render public service was one compelling factor in bringing me, and hundreds of young fellows like me, to Washington in 1933. It was as if we were responding, twenty-eight years early, to Jack Kennedy's great challenge: "Ask not what your country can do for you; ask what you can do for your country."

Some years ago a former student of mine, born long after Franklin Roosevelt's death, spoke gloomily to me about his generation's lack of focus and ambition for anything more than a good income. I suggested that his was not the first group of young college graduates to feel no "call," no excitement about the future, no certainty about what they wanted to do.

This did not satisfy him; after all, for *him* it was the first. Then he burst out: "I wish I understood about the young men in the New Deal! I have a feeling that they caught a glimpse of something wonderful, and were somehow uplifted by it; but why this was, and what made them tick, I do not know." I wished that I could tell him but, pressed for time, I couldn't— then. Now I can try, belatedly, to give him a once-young man's answer, and leave the rest to poets and to him.

Some years ago I started to write an article about the eager,

---

*However, in many ways the twenties (not the thirties) and the eighties were alike, and this was one of them. I recall a college student who, in his senior class yearbook in 1927, wrote that his intended career was "public service." The poor guy was mercilessly ridiculed for this by his classmates.

diligent, and ambitious young lawyers who crowded into Washington in 1933. I got only as far as one long metaphorical paragraph. This I have shown to two friends, economist John Kenneth Galbraith and political scientist and historian James MacGregor Burns. Mention of these gentlemen makes me wonder what the magic is in three-word names. When I entered politics should I have called myself Thomas Hopkinson Eliot, instead of using just the initial? I didn't, perhaps because of a youthful scunner against triple nomenclature derived from my family's dislike of Senator Henry Cabot Lodge the elder. He was the man who led the fight against the United States' joining the League of Nations. Of him my grandfather once said to me: "Henry Cabot Lodge is not the meanest man I have ever known. His father was."

Probably I'm whimsically straying from the subject of the New Deal because I'm stalling for time and mustering my courage to disagree with Professor Galbraith, with whose opinions I rarely differ. He did not find my metaphorical paragraph appropriate. Professor Burns did. So do I; so here it is.

Among the fauna that frequented the banks of the Potomac in the early nineteen-thirties were some very large and highly articulate animals. Chief among them, of course, was the Lion; other folk, but not I, called him the King of Beasts. He was of mammoth dimensions, and presided over a group of sizable quadrupeds. Some of these, being literate, kept diaries or wrote memoirs, so that we know what the world was like from their point of view. Their leader was too busy to record his daily doings, but history has done that for him; one biographer, indeed, has determined that he was not only a Lion but also a Fox.* All in all, we know what Washington was like—looking from the top down. It's unlikely that we could see much, looking from the bottom up. As in a real forest, the multitudinous insect life helps to maintain the balance of nature, but few of the ants or grubs can see much of what is going on. In the nineteen-thirties in Washington, however, there was

*James MacGregor Burns, *Roosevelt: The Lion and the Fox* (New York: Harcourt, Brace, 1956).

an unusually large and active number of middle-sized animals. Among these, especially vigorous, was a bevy of beavers— sometimes sharp-toothed, always busy, forever eager. They moved about among the trees and glimpsed, at least, the forest. I was a beaver.

Why had I, and so many other beavers—let's call them youthful lawyers—hastened to Washington in the early days of the New Deal? Not, I think, out of economic necessity: the Depression was at its worst, but we were not unemployed. We had been successful, or fairly so, at law school and could still get jobs in the private sector. Nor for lucre: I took a cut, from $1800 to $1700 a year, when I moved from a Buffalo law firm to the Department of Labor. What, then?

Perhaps, to some degree, a desire for power or at least influence. Washington had suddenly become the power center of the country, and even those in middle-level positions would perhaps become advisers to the wielders of power. To a larger degree, we came to Washington because that's where the action was. We wanted to be involved. But for some, at least, the most important thing was what we wanted to be involved in: our perhaps ingenuous conviction that we were part of a great and noble effort to serve the country, and especially to serve the millions of our fellow citizens who desperately needed help. This was certainly a motive that made some young New Dealers tick. And the realization that recovery from Depression and despair, and reform so that these need not recur, could be achieved by a government in which we played small but active parts was perhaps the "glimpse of something wonderful" to which my young questioner referred.

So far as I know, no ex-beaver has shared with a later generation, in print, at length, and in detail, his experience in those heady, exhilarating days.* I refer to the years from 1933 through 1937, the quadrennium of peaceful revolution that

---

*In *The Making of the New Deal* (Cambridge: Harvard University Press, 1983), edited by Katie Louchheim, there are fifty interviews with men and women who worked in Washington, in various capacities, during the Roosevelt years. Their reminiscences, however, while often colorful, are decidedly brief, averaging only six pages in print apiece.

changed America. Granted that without Roosevelt and his official and unofficial cabinet great change might have come, though more gradually and in different guise. Granted that without a horde of unsung civil servants the new programs might have been strangled by inefficiency. The fact remains that broad principles on the one hand, and dutiful routine on the other, do not by themselves create a revolutionary program. Between the top policymakers and the routineers must always be the second-echelon advisers and administrators, whose grasp of detail shapes the policy and makes it workable. Often this second-echelon group includes lawyers. And never in this group, I suppose, have the lawyers been so dominant, or so young, as they were in the New Deal.

The good historians of the period realize this. They could not peruse old newspaper files of the thirties without noting how often the young lawyers were referred to—frequently anonymously and often abusively or derisively. (A Philadelphia attorney, for reasons which I forget, once called me a snapping turtle—a zoological misnomer.) They were lumped together: they were "Corcoran and Cohen," or they were "happy hot dogs."

Now, it is true that Thomas G. Corcoran zealously and skillfully recruited fellow graduates of the Harvard Law School for legal positions in various Federal agencies.* It's true, too, that he collaborated with the dedicated Benjamin V. Cohen (then an old man of forty) in framing some major legislation. And it is also a fact that Professor Felix Frankfurter, of Harvard, after whom the "happy hot dogs" were named, had long urged his students to enter public service and had recommended some for governmental posts.

But whether or not he was a friend of Corcoran or a favorite of Frankfurter, the usual New Deal lawyer did not remain in bondage to either one. He was, typically, a man of considerable

---

*Operating at first out of a legal post in the Reconstruction Finance Corporation, Corcoran eventually and semi-officially became a presidential assistant, speech-writer, lobbyist, and spokesman.

ability and even more self-confidence, and no one could keep him on a leash. In the New Deal areas that my "turf" comprised, the second echelon was composed mainly of young lawyers with a Harvard tinge, and slightly older economists from the stable of John R. Commons of Wisconsin. The attorneys, more ebullient and less contemplative, usually grabbed the ball and ran with it. In retrospect, I wonder that the sober economists and "public administration" veterans did not feel more resentment than they sometimes showed.

There is a danger in writing about the New Deal lawyers: the peril of oversimple generalization. These young men were individuals, idealistically dedicated or crassly on the make or both. They had their different interests and dissimilar ambitions. Yet there were so many of them with so often a common educational background* that is was natural for critical journalists to lump them together. This tendency continued: witness the title of a book about the Alger Hiss case, *A Generation on Trial.* My effort now cannot be to sort them out. The disparities and complications are too many, and anyway I am unsuited for the role of biographer of my friends of long ago. But I can make a start by being autobiographical.

At the age of twenty-six, one year out of Harvard Law School, I became the number-two man** in the Office of the Solicitor of the U.S. Department of Labor. A year later I became counsel for President Roosevelt's Committee on Economic Security, and so was the principal draftsman of the "Economic Security Bill" that, changed in numerous details and renamed and renumbered by Congress, became the Social Security Act. That law established a Social Security Board to administer most of its far-reaching programs; in the fall of

---

*At a farewell luncheon given by his staff upon his retirement as general counsel of the Securities and Exchange Commission, John J. Burns began his speech with the words: "Fellow alumni of the Harvard Law School. . . ."

**Officially, I started as junior attorney and was promoted to senior attorney; with the Solicitor's permission I signed official letters as "Associate Solicitor." A critical congressman once challenged me: "There is no such title in the budget." "No, there isn't," I replied, "the actual title for my rank is 'senior attorney,' but wouldn't it sound kind of silly? I'm twenty-six." He was mollified.

1935 I became the Board's general counsel, going on unpaid leave two years later and resigning when I announced my candidacy for Congress in June 1938.

That's the bare outline. I am able to flesh it out, not because I have an especially good memory, but because I was a prolific letter-writer. My mother and my friend Richard C. Berresford of New York, both of whom died years ago, kept the letters I wrote them, including many from Washington in the New Deal years. These old letters eventually came into my hands; and in old files I have found, also, a few months' worth of a dictated diary (a factual record with disappointingly few opinions) that I kept in 1934.

The letters, roughly weekly to my mother and five or six a year to my friend, are not memorable examples of the epistolary art. Even if they were, they would bore the general reader because they are naturally full of personal allusions, the state of my health, the marriages of relatives, the fortunes of the Boston Braves (*sic transit . . . !*), and the like. Even as an autobiographical record they are misleading, for, in writing to my mother, I tailored my letters somewhat to her interests. Thus, they include an inordinate amount about not my concerns but those of my brother Charles, who was executive officer of the National Resources Planning Board. Charles, a generous brother and a devoted son, was, alas, a poor correspondent. For my mother's sake, I tried to fill the gap.

Nevertheless, the letters have enough in them to remind me vividly of those days of strenuous labor, normal fun, occasional frustration, and the astonishingly confident assumption of responsibility. Not always, to be sure, do they remind me of anything at all. In rereading them, I have been sometimes amazed to learn that I had met this man or that, had dined with so-and-so and played tennis with another. Still, most written references do refresh the inward eye. And although I was brought up on Edward Everett Hale's instruction to "look forward and not back," the present backward glance to me seems justified. As I have said, much of the New Deal came to stay, and among those who established it were the young men of whom I was one. The present configuration of our governmental process is largely an outgrowth of the New Deal or an adverse reaction to it. And every economic recession makes one realize that if that recession deepens, the "crisis management" of the thirties will be only too relevant.

Now I'm in my eighties. Most of the New Deal lawyers I knew and worked with from 1933 to 1937 are dead and gone. None of them has published a book about the New Deal. I'm one of the few survivors. If none of my remaining contemporaries rushes into print (and I doubt if anyone will do so) this little volume will be the last account of the great days of the New Deal to be written by an actor in that historic drama.

I arrived in Washington eager and impressionable. I remember driving one cool, sunny morning to a spot on the Mall from which one had a good view of both the Capitol and the Lincoln Memorial, taking a long breath and saying out loud: "What a lucky guy you are, Eliot!" The move to Washington was easy and comfortable. While looking for housing I could, and did, stay with the family of my brother Charles, who at that time was finishing his term as director of city planning for the District of Columbia. The search for housing was easy, too; after all, the Depression was going strong and the real estate market was soft indeed. The only challenge was to find the right congenial bachelors with whom to share a house. That also was easy to meet, for the city was swimming with newly arrived, young, single government lawyers.

I knew so many of them that I dare now to make some generalized comments about them. Most—I think almost all—had one thing in common. They worked hard. I can't fairly describe the atmosphere of New Deal Washington without emphasizing that fact. And one thing that many young New Dealers shared, whether they were starry-eyed or merely hungry for personal advancement, was joy in the work they were doing. It was absorbing, mentally. It was exciting, because of the scope of its subject and, at least at first, the glamour surrounding it. Of course, a portrait painter would not have thrilled to the task of drafting statutes, and a cynical poet might have said "So what?" when told he was about to confer with a cabinet minister. But I am writing about lawyers who were technically trained for the jobs they did, and who came to Washington not because they had to but because they wanted to.

I, for one, had been raised in a politically conscious household, and believed public service to offer an opportunity for the most satisfying career possible—if the conditions were right. I missed the famous "hundred days," when the first New Deal legislation was rushed through Congress, but that period was not half over before it seemed to me that the conditions were indeed right. On July 12, 1933, having just been admitted to the New York bar, I joined the Office of the Solicitor of the U.S. Department of Labor. The Solicitor was my college and law school friend Charles E. Wyzanski, Jr. He was twenty-seven; I was twenty-six. For the next four years, the positions that I held and the work that absorbed and stirred me concerned labor and social security. Inevitably, then, this book must be primarily about those subjects.

To be sure, the day's work in a single office in one department could be strangely and wonderfully varied. Here is my dictated diary entry for March 8, 1934:

> Wrote memorandum for Colonel MacCormack concerning immigration bills up for vote on March 29.
> Drafted directive, for Secretary, on disposition of useless papers.
> Walker, of Petroleum Board, called for statistical data to be used in Supreme Court brief.
> Conferred with Lubin about the anthracite situation and then went to the White House to brief Louis Howe who had asked for information about it.
> Lunched with Dr. Leiserson and Wyzanski, discussing the Labor Disputes bill and possible further witnesses for the Wagner-Lewis bill.
> Wrote Felix Morley [of the *Washington Post*] about his editorial, and Mrs. August Belmont, also about the Wagner-Lewis bill.

Long conference on Wagner-Lewis bill with representatives of the National Consumers League, the Y.W.C.A., the League of Women Voters, the National Federation of Teachers, and the National Council of Jewish Women.

Drafting session, with Levitt [Department of Justice] and Hackworth [State Department] on the Nationality Code.

Dined out, and went to a ball."

Two of these items can be dismissed with a few words. The "disposition of useless papers" is hardly a breathtaking issue, though for many years it was important enough for Congress to have a standing committee on the subject. The session with Messrs. Hackworth and Levitt was more significant. Or at least the matter was more time-consuming, both before and after March 8, 1934. The preparation of a new "Nationality Code" proceeded extremely slowly, with Mr. Levitt* providing many new ideas of varying worth, the State Department representatives looking shocked and pained by his proposals, and I being alternately amused and bored.

I was a member of that drafting committee because in those days the Immigration and Naturalization Service was part of the Department of Labor. (It was later shifted to the Justice Department.) The protracted conferences continued, intermittently, for years. Long before the proposed "code" was completed and appeared, in altered form, on the statute books, I had left the committee and was concentrating on one or the other of the two major subjects mentioned in that diary entry.

One of these was labor—labor disputes and labor legislation. These are the subjects of Chapter 3. In this diary entry there are intimations that for a young man of twenty-six the handling of such matters could bring a glow of surprised excitement. Louis McHenry Howe was an irritable gnome (as well as a wise adviser), but to be talking at the White House with the president's right-hand man was faintly glamorous.

---

*As I recall it, Albert Levitt later became a federal judge in the U.S.–owned Virgin Islands. I was told that there he deliberately made no friends because he thought if he did, his impartiality as a judge would be jeopardized. He made headlines in 1937 by vociferously opposing the nomination of Hugo Black to the U.S. Supreme Court. He was an interesting, irritating, odd man.

And there was glamour of a different sort in even epistolary contact with the public-spirited former actress Eleanor Robson Belmont. She was in her fifties then, as beautiful a woman as I ever hope to see. My letter to her concerned social security— more specifically, a plan to promote the passage of state unemployment insurance laws through the enactment, by Congress, of the Wagner-Lewis bill. This bill, a year or more later, became the law of the land through its inclusion in the Social Security Act. The preparation, passage, and administration of that act are the subjects of Chapters 4, 5, and 6.

Here, however, the final item should not be overlooked. "Dined out, and went to a ball." Were the young New Dealers, then, forever dressing for dinner and dancing into the wee hours? Such a frivolous picture of them was never broadcast by their critics, nor could it well have been, for it was not the case. White ties, it was generally assumed, were worn by young men only if they were in the State Department—in which case they were probably not New Dealers at all.

The real New Dealers were not playboys in their own eyes. Life was real and life was earnest. But the journalistic picture of them, influenced by the press lords' hostility to Roosevelt, was chiefly that of eager, wet-behind-the-ears, dogmatic radicals, planning and plotting at an endless series of cocktail parties. Less scrupulous critics equated "radicals" with "communists," calling Tom Corcoran's residence "The Little Red House in Georgetown." This last bit of alleged political history persisted for a long time, confirmation of it seeming to appear in the late forties and early fifties, the Joe McCarthy era, when it crept into respectable history books. Not Roosevelt haters but New Deal apologists of a younger generation came to assume with somewhat patronizing sympathy that the bright young men of the thirties had gravitated toward Marxism. This, they thought, was only natural under the circumstances, and those idealistic dupes of communism were more to be pitied than scorned.

For a time this preposterous notion that New Dealers were

pervasively (and of course understandably, if you are a truly understanding observer) inclined toward communism became part of the nation's political folklore. It was, indeed, a central part of the Republicans' presidential campaign in 1952, thanks to the inclusion of Richard M. Nixon on the ticket. Dramatized by the Hiss conviction, it was given further force by a few well-publicized "disclosures." Yet if all the evidence, credible and untrustworthy alike, is lumped together, there is still no indication that the great changes in domestic policy in 1933–37 were in any way, shape, or manner influenced by communist dogma or by communists.

In that period, of course, a person could be a communist and still not be at all alarming. The Soviet Union was a weak and backward country, and in the United States the futility of the Communist Party had been shown by its utter failure to gain popular support in the depths of the Depression. And so it seemed in Washington—or anyway it seemed to me—that if anyone was a communist, it was probably because he was a soft-hearted idealist distressed by the suffering of the unemployed, or an adventurous fellow out for some intellectual exercise, or a psychiatric case. It was further assumed, at least by some of us, that this man and that man (or, in a couple of cases, that woman) were communists and it would be a poor idea to put them into responsible positions—not for fear of red revolution, but because they were dogmatic and unpredictable, like the party line, and exceedingly hard to get along with.

Lee Pressman, for instance, was a communist in this period, during which, for a short time, he was employed in the Agriculture Department. He did not admit it for nearly twenty years, but some other young men, myself included, took it for granted. Not everyone disliked him because of it, but even those, again including me, who considered him brilliant successfully opposed his ambition to succeed Wyzanski as Solicitor of Labor. During the period of which I write, Nathan Witt joined the staff of the National Labor Relations Board. He was generally believed to be a least a "fellow traveler," as was an early member of that board (or its predecessor), a gentleman with an impeccable business background until he was psychoanalyzed and began calling his agency, unintentionally, the "Sexual Relations Board." But these two men did not rule the NLRB, nor did they fashion the legislation that created it, the National Labor Relations Act of 1935.

I have searched my memory and my written records, and find in them next to nothing about communism in New Deal Washington.* There was a stir in the Labor Department about the expulsion from our shores of the left-wing British politician John Strachey; I wrote that to drive such a distinguished visitor away was nonsensical. The "Little Red Rider," a Congressional amendment that prohibited teaching about communism in the District of Columbia's public schools, was "ridiculous" and should be repealed. And in one letter I mentioned being amused that the draftsmen of an early version of the Securities and Exchange Act, including one of my housemates, were being called "reds" by the irresponsibly vehement opposition. That is all.

In no letter did I mention Alger Hiss, and if I had it wouldn't have been as a communist. I made his acquaintance through his younger brother, Donald Hiss, my law school classmate. Alger was a very able lawyer, on friendly terms with many of the young New Dealers but not really one of them. After a stay in the Agricultural Adjustment Administration (AAA), where he survived the "purge" of alleged radicals, he was running on a different track from most of us. We were developing action programs on the domestic front. He was working for the Nye committee, whose investigation of armament profits led to the

---

*I should point out that before going to Washington I had been an Al Smith Democrat, and had suffered no hardship in the Depression. In 1931 Professor Frankfurter once asked me, abruptly, "Are you a conservative or a liberal?" I answered, "I think I'm probably a conservative liberal." On both sides, what an inane exercise in semantics! At least the vagueness of my reply correctly revealed a lack of theoretical dogmatism. The only theory to which I was consciously committed was the principle of individual liberty as expressed in the Bill of Rights and the Fourteenth Amendment. Today I would add my conviction that government should be not only "of" and "by," but "*for*" the people.

passage of the Neutrality Act (an odd occupation for any communist in those days of Hitler's threats against Russia). It seemed fitting that he should eventually go the State Department. Almost the only thing that Whittaker Chambers said about Hiss that rang true, in my skeptical ears, was the descriptive word "stuffy." Yet Alger Hiss, as I knew him, was much better than just stuffy: he was a charming and kindly gentleman.

Now all of the foregoing may indicate merely that I was a singularly naive young man, blind to what was going on around me. Maybe so. But if so, three factors causing my blindness likewise afflicted the majority of my colleagues. The first of these factors was that we were enormously occupied with the jobs in front of us. The second was that most of us, without a doubt, wanted to get ahead fast, and immersion in Marxism was hardly a good way to further one's ambitions. The third was that we had little or no interest in dialectics. The typical young New Deal lawyer was in his policy a pragmatist, in his daily work a technician, and in his spare time a bachelor seeking exercise, relaxation, and romance.

Certainly I do not recall earnest conversations about communism or any other ideology in any of the three bachelor households in which I lived. The first of these was a brownstone on 18th Street, less than a ten minutes' walk from the ancient Labor Department building at G and 17th. Among my housemates were Telford Taylor, a boyhood friend as well as a law school classmate, and Francis Shea, whom I had come to know and like during my few months of legal practice in Buffalo. Shea was then working for the Agricultural Adjustment Administration, one of a brilliant legal staff that was denounced as radical and was "purged" in a bitter internecine battle over the division of benefit payments between landowners and sharecroppers. A victim of that purge, Frank Shea nevertheless survived in the New Deal, eventually becoming Assistant Attorney-General.

Taylor in 1933 was supposedly employed in the Interior Department, but somehow (such was the fine disregard for organizational charts in those heady days) was busy with an even younger lawyer, I. N. P. Stokes, in drafting the initial version of a bill that became the Securities Exchange Act of 1934. Soon he moved to a post-purge spot in the Agricultural Adjustment Administration, and thence to the general counselship of the Federal Communications Commission. In the course of World War II he became a general in Army Intelligence, and was one of the prosecutors at the Nuremberg trials.

As far as I was concerned, Shea and Taylor were fine housemates in all but one respect. Half a century later Taylor remembered this when he said: "I lived with a group of bachelors in a house on 18th Street. Francis Shea liked to sit up late and drink and talk. Tom Eliot would be up there trying to sleep. We'd hear him coughing and slamming doors. [But] in the daytime we got along well."* Oh, come on, Telford! Frank liked not only to talk but to sing, and you played the piano at all hours. I had good reason to slam doors.

One evening, we had a self-invited guest for dinner, a very large third-year student at the Harvard Law School. Normally talkative, this young man sat silent all through the meal, while Shea defended the killing of little pigs under the agricultural program, Taylor denounced the chicanery of Wall Street and the Stock Exchange's head, Richard Whitney, and I described General Johnson, director of the National Recovery Administration, as an "irresponsible juvenile." Finally the talk stopped and our guest opened his mouth. "This sounds like a pretty good racket, " he said. "How does one muscle into it?"

In June 1934, the marriage of another of my housemates, Alexander Hawes, broke up the original group. For the next two years I shared other houses in Georgetown, each time with four other men—again, all of them New Deal lawyers. No, that is not quite correct. One housemate, James Rowe, was not a young New Dealer in 1934; he was the last secretary-companion of retired Justice Oliver Wendell Holmes, Jr. And

*Louchheim, ed., *The Making of the New Deal*, p. 241.

in the following year my roommate was David Riesman, Justice Louis D. Brandeis's secretary.* Dave was a brilliant lawyer— allegedly, he had graduated from the Harvard Law School with the highest grades since those of Brandeis himself—but he did not join the New Deal. Eventually he gained fame as a sociologist and author of *The Lonely Crowd*.

Rowe, in contrast, did stay on as a New Deal lawyer, and after a few years became an administrative assistant to President Roosevelt. (Much later, with no official position, he was a close friend and adviser of President Johnson.) But it was when he was with Justice Holmes that he did me a great favor—me, and my immediate boss at the Department of Labor, Charles E. Wyzanski, Jr. Both Charlie and I had great admiration for the ninety-two-year-old Holmes; neither of us had met him. Jim Rowe invited us to call on him.

He was still magnificently handsome. His flashing eyes re-minded me of how, as a law student, I used to take a seat in the Langdell Hall library right under my uncle Charles Hopkin-son's great full-length portrait of Justice Holmes: I knew that with those eyes gazing down from the wall at me, I would have to concentrate on my studies!

The justice offered cigars to Wyzanski and me. We declined. Jim Rowe spoke up: "You didn't offer me one, Judge." "Oh," said Holmes, "would you take one?" "Yes, sir." "That," said Holmes, "is why I wouldn't offer you one." Later, his brow low-ering, he spoke of my grandfather, Charles W. Eliot. "He wrote that letter to a lady in Beverly Farms," he said, "way back, way back, when he was just an instructor at Harvard, not yet pres-ident of the college, and I was a freshman. He wrote that the freshman class was rather jackety." His voice rose. "He called us *jackety!*" Jim asked, "What does jackety mean, Judge?" Irrit-ably, Holmes replied, "Oh, clad in short jackets—juvenile, I suppose." More calmly he continued: "However, he did many good things and on his ninetieth birthday I wrote to tell him so." He turned to me with a look of triumph. "So, then I got a

---

*This position is now called "law clerk."

letter from old Eliot. It was *magisterial,* I thought." Revenge at last!

Those bachelor households that I've mentioned needed help: few of us could cook, and none had time to cook. In Georgetown, we were lucky indeed; we hired a young woman, Marie Atkins, to come in by the day—for nine dollars a week. (This was a dollar higher than what she had been earning at a house across the street.) She was terrific—smart, funny, and thoughtful. One of my housemates that year was Paul Herzog (whom she always called "Herdoz"), later chairman of the National Labor Relations Board. I was alone one warm evening when the telephone rang. It was Marie: "Mr. Eliot, it's starting to rain. Mr. Herdoz's bed is out on the porch. It'll get wet. Move it in, quick!" I obeyed orders. Another time, I came home to find the living room filled with steam. I was late for a black-tie date, so I dashed upstairs, changed, and dashed out again. A few minutes later, my housemate Ed Rhetts (later ambassador to Liberia) arrived. Through the steam he shouted for Marie. 'Hasn't anyone been here? Was Mr. Eliot here?" "Oh, yes," she said. "He was here. All he did was run up and down. I ask him what to do, and all he does is yell 'Get the plumber, Marie, get the plumber!' Might just as well have been talking to a rabbit!"

Actually, I couldn't often dress up and go out for the evening—there was too much work to be done. So much, in fact, that few evenings could be spent in either revelry or philosophical conversation. For example, entries in the diary that I kept in 1934 show that in one week in March, on every night but one I was "home at midnight" from the office or from evening hearings on Capitol Hill. And a letter to my parents in 1935, shortly after the Supreme Court invalidated the National Recovery Administration (NRA), shows that there was little time for either philandering or philosophizing:

> For the last ten days I have been:
> 1. Rewriting the Guffey Coal bill, trying to get it into shape worthy of F. D.'s endorsement. At present it is a vicious bill, but he wants to pass it in some form.

2. With Gerry Reilly,* drawing a bill to make government contracts provide that contractors will pay fair wages.

3. Organizing and to a large extent "putting over" the Interstate Compact Conference here, Harry Parkman [a Massachusetts state senator] presiding. With Jim Landis, he and I worked out a proposal for Federal action [to encourage interstate compacts] and got F. D. to "direct a study" of it along the lines we indicated. Miss Perkins [the Secretary of Labor] was swell.

4. Getting through the Budget Bureau and then the White House a recommended appropriation of $600,000 additional for the Department [of Labor]. The President has boosted this publicly. Saunders, the budget man in the Department, did a lot of the work on that as well, but it was my idea that we should do it and could get it!

5. Kept in touch with the Social Security bill and prepared answers to proposed amendments which will be offered on the floor of the Senate.

6. Saw the Secretary countless times about the NRA business [the Supreme Court's decision declaring the National Industrial Recovery Act unconstitutional], and also interviewed numerous people about panaceas.

7. Did the regular routine work of the Solicitor of the Department. [Wyzanski was in Europe.]

That letter was, obviously, what might be called a self-serving document, for I wanted my parents to be proud of me—but it does suggest, truthfully, that I was keeping busy. Too many other letters report episodes of temporary exhaustion. But still others strike a happier note. "All work and no play make Jack a dull boy—an original idea!" I wrote: So for a moment let's turn to the recreation that made life livable for me and many like me.

Able-bodied men need exercise. I knew this. Sometimes it was impossible, and I had to comfort myself—or my mother— by noting that I walked to work and back: from Georgetown it was one and two-thirds miles each way. But more often I mention games of squash, and on weekends baseball (softball, surely) and touch football—a surprising amount of the last, for the Kennedys had not yet arrived and made that game popu-

*Gerard D. Reilly, later a member of the National Labor Relations Board and still later a judge of the District of Columbia Court of Appeals.

lar. There was tennis, too, though games often had to be canceled because I could not get away from the office until after dark. And on February 5, 1934, I wrote: "More and more snow! This is a most surprising place. I had thought it was tropical. Yesterday [a Sunday], we made the most of it, and had a grand time tobogganing at the Burlings' and later playing prisoners' base—'we' being chiefly young gov't lawyers with a mixture of married women and debutantes. About 30 for lunch—hot stew and sandwiches and fruit."

Under this heading of "recreation" I think it's fair to place not only sport but occasions that helped to provide the glamour which was such an important part of a young New Dealer's life. In May 1934, "luncheon at a fine big farm in Virginia [Wolf Trap Farm], the Jouett Shouses', where Harry Hopkins had an interesting discussion with Jim Landis [holder of several high public offices and later dean of Harvard Law School]." I pause here to express my surprise, for this is but one of many mentions of the Shouses' hospitality in my letters.

Surprise, for two reasons: first, I have no present recollection of most of these recorded occasions and, second, how could Jouett Shouse tolerate me or I him? He hated the president. He was an ex-congressman from Kansas, who after the debacle of 1928 had become chairman of the executive committee of the Democratic National Committee. He wanted to be "permanent chairman" of the party's national convention in 1932. Sensing that he would use that post to try to prevent Roosevelt's nomination, F. D. R. maneuvered successfully to block his selection. In the mid-thirties Shouse, Al Smith, and some big-business Democrats and Republicans formed the American Liberty League, whose clear objective was to thwart and indeed destroy the New Deal: as Al Smith put it, to "throw the New Deal out of the window three letters at a time." Shouse became the League's president.

I can think of only two reasons that I should have been socially acceptable to him. One was that in the spring of 1932 I had invited him to be the keynote speaker at Harvard's mock

Democratic convention. He came, we hit it off immediately, and he was probably pleased to find that—at that time—I was, like him, a "Smith man." The other was that his wife, Katherine, was surely more liberal than he was. She was the daughter of Boston merchant Lincoln Filene, a big-business man if you will, but not a conservative one, and a close friend of Justice Brandeis. Anyway, I do have a couple of pleasant memories of the Shouses' hospitality, though I'm still startled by its apparent frequency.

In one of my letters home, I mentioned my surprise at the vehemence of Jouett Shouse's hatred of Roosevelt. As his guest, I felt unable to rush to the president's defense. I could and did try tactfully (I think) to indicate my general disagreement with my host's opinions, and at the same time to express guarded agreement with some of his minor criticisms, such as Roosevelt's skill ("duplicity," Shouse called it) in making people believe that he approved of their ideas when he actually disapproved.*

One did not have to know Jouett Shouse to be fully aware of the fact that many people, most of them rich or decidedly well-off, sincerely hated Roosevelt. Right in Washington was a newspaper, the *Times-Herald*, that engaged in constant denunciation of his programs and policies. But beginning in 1934, I think, with the enactment of the law regulating the stock market, criticism of policies was replaced by hatred of the man himself. Arthur M. Schlesinger, Jr., has described this as "a disease of the *rentier* class. Depression and the New Deal had knocked the pinnings from under them; accustomed to security, they were

---

*Years later, I saw an example of this. In January 1941, when I was a newly elected congressman, I dined at the White House. Among the guests was Frank Knox, Secretary of the Navy. He suggested that a large ocean liner, the *Normandie*, be sent to England to pick up English children fleeing the blitz and other refugees from Hitler's Europe. Then, he said, we should falsely tip off the Germans that the ship was transporting top secrets and top British statesmen to the United States! On its return voyage a Nazi submarine would sink it. The outcry in America would be so great that Congress would be ready and even eager to declare war. President Roosevelt's response, uttered with seeming enthusiasm, was "That's an idea, Frank, that's an idea!" (I'm glad to say that on that occasion Mrs. Roosevelt had the last word: "It's a *terrible* idea!")

adrift; accustomed to power, they were frightened as new forces boiled up from the lower depths. Everything they stood for seemed under mortal attack—and, worst of all, the man leading the attack was one of their own."* "A traitor to his class" became a constantly recurring descriptive phrase.

The hostility of the small but wealthy and still influential minority took on increased venom in 1935, with the enactment of the National Labor Relations Act that denied employers the right to run their companies as they saw fit, without having to bargain and share authority with greedy, obstreperous labor unions. And it certainly was not reduced by Roosevelt's own reaction to it. Addressing the nation over the radio, he heaped scorn on "economic royalists." Accepting renomination for the presidency in 1936, he said that in his first term "the forces of greed met their match"; in his second term "they will meet their master."

I remember a dinner at a men's club in, I think, 1937. A very friendly, personable business man trotted out all the usual anti-Roosevelt clichés. After dinner I asked him, privately, why he hated the president so, when his own business, which had barely escaped bankruptcy in 1932, was now highly successful. Hadn't the New Deal made this possible? He looked surprised, muttered, "I suppose so," and then burst out: "He shouldn't call us names!"

But that was in Boston, when I was paying a brief visit to my parents in Cambridge. Back in Washington, I seriously doubt that young New Dealers spent much, if any, time listening to and arguing with rich right-wing Roosevelt-haters. We knew that they existed, and that they were outnumbered by the humbler folk who were helped by the New Deal and thanked and sometimes really loved the president. We were also aware of critics not from the right but from the left, critics who felt that the New Deal had not gone nearly far enough: it was merely shoring up the capitalist system, when much more fun-

*Schlesinger, *The Coming of the New Deal* (Boston: Houghton Mifflin, 1959), p. 569.

damental reform was needed. We disliked, but were not dismayed by, diatribes in the *Times-Herald;* more disturbing was the other kind of opposition, personified by Huey Long, the Louisiana despot, whose slogans were "share the wealth" and "every man a king!"

Of the eventual real enemy, Adolf Hitler, I do not remember much, if any, discussion or argument. For one thing, we were all—at least everyone I knew—anti-Nazi. For another, we were immersed in matters of domestic policy, not foreign policy. Not until the British and French allowed Hitler to occupy the Rhineland with impunity in 1936 was there much talk of the possibility of war. In contrast, some of us were interested by the hearings before the Nye Committee, investigating munitions makers ("merchants of death" was the stock phrase for them) and war profiteers. But this too was secondary or peripheral; our concerns were right here, in the Depression-ridden U.S.A. When I say "our" concerns I refer to the young New Deal lawyers; the Nye Committee and the Neutrality Act it spawned were very much the concern of Lois Jameson, the lady I married in October 1936, for she was the assistant to the director of the Women's International League for Peace and Freedom.

In 1937, Lois and I gave a number of small Sunday night supper parties at our apartment on 15th Street. I must have chauvinistically controlled the guest lists for those parties, for I recall only one guest who was involved in foreign policy: namely, Alger Hiss. Even he was a lawyer, as were most of the men who came to supper. Among our guests were Solicitor General Stanley Reed, Assistant Attorney-General Robert H. Jackson, and Senator Hugo L. Black. All three of them were to become justices of the Supreme Court.

I have no idea how we happened to invite the Reeds. I have no recollection of working with him, nor does my wife remember meeting his wife. But we must have had some contact with one or both of them, for they accepted our invitation. Reed was a kindly, modest man, unsure of himself—he agonized when his position, that of the government's chief advocate, required him to argue important cases before the Supreme Court—and later, as a justice of that Court, he was a reliable, moderate, and undistinguished liberal judge.

Bob Jackson was something else. In early 1937 I saw a lot of him, for he and Wyzanski and I were working together preparing the government's briefs in the social security cases that were to be argued that spring before the Supreme Court. Jackson had a first-rate, incisive mind, an eloquent pen, and a belligerently liberal faith. But as time passed, his attractive personality became warped by overwhelming ambition. He wanted to be elected president in 1940. This desire came to Roosevelt's ears before Roosevelt had decided to run in 1940 himself, for an unprecedented third term. The president arranged to let Bob Jackson "test the waters" by making a series of speeches to influential audiences. But Jackson's subject, enforcement of the anti-trust laws, was less than thrilling, and his speech-making tour, in theatrical parlance, laid an egg.

His ambition (he didn't conceal it; he was always expressing it to influential people who had the president's ear, such as Secretary of the Interior Ickes) turned, and successfully, to obtaining a seat on the Supreme Court. He wrote numerous memorable liberal opinions in important cases: as I've said, he had an eloquent pen. But again, ambition intervened, souring his relationship with his brethren on the Court and impairing his reputation. He wanted to be Chief Justice, and when he was passed over, he publicly blamed his colleagues, especially Justice Black, for blocking his appointment. He died soon thereafter, a disappointed and disappointing man.

As for Hugo Black, in 1937 a senator from Alabama, my wife and I knew him because of his relationship with our close friends, those great Alabama liberals Clifford and Virginia Durr.* Black's wife was Virginia Durr's sister. The senator him-

---

*An excellent biography of Clifford Durr is Johnson, *The Conscience of a Lawyer* (Tuscaloosa: University of Alabama Press, 1990), and good reading, too, is Virginia Durr's autobiography, *Outside the Magic Circle* (Tuscaloosa: University of Alabama Press, 1986).

self was known as a fighting liberal who, politically, could "play rough," though in personal demeanor he was smooth and courtly. He was the first of our three guests to reach the Supreme Court, his appointment being an example of Roosevelt's political skill. The president had just lost the "Court-packing fight," his ill-conceived idea to increase the number of justices on the Court so that he could name judges who would vote to sustain New Deal laws. The reaction to this plan was so adverse that, when a vacancy on the bench was created by Justice Van Devanter's resignation, it seemed likely that any liberal nominee to fill that vacancy would have a very hard time getting confirmed by the Senate. But Roosevelt dispelled that concern by nominating Black—a senator, a "member of the club"— knowing that the Senate would not reject one of its own.

Black's qualifications seemed minimal, but he turned out to be one of the most influential justices in the history of the Court. His intellectual force often appeared to dominate the decision-making process. But my wife and I would not have expected that when we had him for supper during his final months as a senator. That evening he did not try to be brainy or brilliant. Though his background was humble, he just exuded the charm of an old-fashioned Southern aristocrat.

Not a future justice in the thirties but a sitting one, not a guest but a host, was another great figure in the history of the Supreme Court. I cherish the memory of occasional and always fascinating "teas" at the apartment of Mr. Justice Brandeis. Probably just to keep the conversation from touching upon questions that might some day come before the Court, he often steered it on to other subjects: the success of Danish dairy cooperatives, for example, or the Massachusetts savings bank life insurance system. He also spoke with great pride of the way he had placed some subordinates in his former law firm in positions best suited to their attributes—positions not beyond their scope, but important enough to demand and elicit the best that was in them. Two decades later when I was a department chairman at Washington University, I remembered Brandeis and like him took pride in pushing a shy, modest under-achiever into responsible and demanding positions within his competence, and then watching him grow in confidence, stature, and reputation. For Brandeis I had unstinted respect, and also gratitude for his kindness as a host at those Monday afternoon teas.

I felt similar respect and gratitude for a hostess: my real chief, the Secretary of Labor, Frances Perkins. After my marriage, Lois and I were more than once her guests; before it, very occasionally with others I lunched or dined with her, but those were working meals that included extended arguments over matters of policy. But her first invitation to me, in November 1933, was to a party—a small dance she was giving for her schoolgirl daughter, Susannah. I was slightly surprised to find myself among a bevy of sixteen-year-old females, and pleased to discover one bright, attractive lady of twenty-two to dance and converse with. I did not realize then, or until Miss Perkins told me years later, that on that occasion the Secretary of Labor was trying her wings as a matchmaker. She thought that it was time I got married, and that she had found the right bride for me. Alas for her plans, I never saw that young lady again.

The foregoing mention of that "small dance" reminds me that in emphasizing the importance of our work to us young lawyers, I may have overlooked some of the social aspects of life in early New Deal Washington. There was time—*sometimes* there was time—to go to concerts or movies or the theater, or more specifically, to take a young woman* to same. What a different, *proper* world it was then! Unmarried men did not live with unmarried women in those pre-pill days. When another fellow and I accompanied two young ladies to a charming sports resort in the West Virginia hills and signed up for two rooms, he and I occupied one of those rooms and the women occupied the other. We never even thought of a different ar-

---

*Tom Eliot wrote, "I thought and still think of them as girls, and . . . that is what they called themselves." And in fact many women of his generation do continue to refer to themselves as girls. The favored current usage is here adopted. —Ed.

rangement. Oh, yes, the young New Dealers of both sexes were normal people, and there were undoubtedly many romances, but about such affairs one and all were demurely discreet.

Incidentally, it should be noted that while among the New Dealers there were numerous females, most of them held secretarial, research, or minor administrative posts. They did not hold law degrees. There were hardly any female lawyers on the scene. There were very few female lawyers, period. In those days, young women who wanted to go to law school were discouraged from doing so: there would be no jobs for them, certainly not in good private law firms. In 1936 I completed the task of hiring ninety lawyers for the Social Security Board's legal staff: just three of them were women. And among the hordes of other applicants for positions on that staff, I don't recall any women at all. However, young ladies did not have to be members of the bar to attract the attention of young legal eagles of the New Deal.

As far as I know, the only feminine counterpart of the several houses filled with bachelors was one which we irreverently called "the Nunnery," where lived six youthful graduates of Smith, Bryn Mawr, and Vassar. This establishment, as I wrote to my mother, "provides frequent female companionship." Again, mentioning the one "nun" whose family she knew: "Betty Ripley and her five housemates provide all the social life you could ask for me. I'm even getting a habit of going over there after work for a glass of sherry (nothing stronger!). Thus does my celibate state get threatened." Threatened indeed it was. Although, just to tease my concerned parent, "which of the girls there I like the best, I know not," I soon admitted that "My interest in the Nunnery suddenly seems to be more clearly defined. One of them is away for two weeks and I haven't found any occasion to go near the place since she left. But [I added, fallaciously] it's not serious." Happily, it was.

The Nunnery was on 34th Street in Washington, but when the heat grew fierce the young ladies moved to a "Summer Nunnery," first a house on Seminary Road on the outskirts of

Alexandria, the next year across the road to a professor's house on the campus of the Episcopal Theological Seminary. These dwellings were cool and comfortable, in a rural setting, ten miles from downtown Washington. It took me nearly half an hour to drive there, over country roads with shortcuts along muddy farm lanes. Today a superhighway takes you to Seminary Road in ten minutes, and the rural aspect has been replaced by high-rise office buildings and condominiums. Progress?

Not all the young ladies were active New Dealers. Lois, as I've mentioned, worked for the Women's International League for Peace and Freedom. Another, far from being a New Dealer, was the assistant of John D. M. Hamilton, chairman of the Republican National Committee and manager of Alfred M. Landon's campaign for president in 1936. Perhaps because of her presence, partisan politics, as far as I can remember, was seldom if ever a subject of discussion at the Nunnery.

All the young women were bright and attractive. All of them had beaux—one of them far too many beaux, as far as I was concerned. If serious romances were few, the Summer Nunnery was in a romantic setting. On one warm evening the residents were treated to a distant, plaintive recorder solo, "Barbara Allen," played by an invisible musician among the trees on the seminary grounds. (He turned out to be John Dreier, later our ambassador to the Organization of American States.) More raucous, on another night, was the arrival of a carload of young lawyers, residents of a bachelor household called Bleagle, like the Summer Nunnery across the Potomac from Washington. They whooped and danced and jovially threatened to burn the house down; they even lit a fire in the grass. A neighbor called the police. When the latter arrived, they were greeted by a loud female cry from an upper story window: "Don't shoot, officer, don't shoot!"

I think the Nunnery residents were central players in a different kind of evening activity—square dancing. Good exercise and good fun, enthusiastically led by an expert do-si-do caller, the aforementioned John Dreier. I remember those lively sessions well; in contrast, I have no recollection of the "ball" mentioned in that diary entry and know that I attended very few of such affairs. As far as I can recall, my confreres and I only rarely changed into a tuxedo, wing collar and all, when we were going out to dinner or to the theater.

Of the ten young lawyers with whom I shared lodgings in the course of a three-year period, I was the third to get married. (Wyzanski, Herzog, Rowe, and Reilly all were ushers at the wedding.) By that time I had a responsible executive position and a good salary. I was still enthusiastic about being a New Dealer; but in 1937 the bloom was beginning to fade from the rose. The Court-packing plan, mentioned above, proved beyond question that our leader, Franklin Roosevelt, was not infallible. Justice Brandeis was consistently advising me, and others like me, to get out of Washington and cultivate our gardens at home. Other circumstances too, as we shall see, propelled me in the same direction. So after four years (I was to return later for another four years, two as a congressman and two as a bureaucrat) I was ready to depart with Lois to seek new adventures in my native Massachusetts. But the glow that permeated that first quadrennium was never fully dispelled; after nearly sixty years, I can still feel its tingling warmth.

Chapter 2

Recovery and Reform

THERE was no place to go but up. On Inauguration Day, March 4, 1933, I walked down Delaware Avenue in Buffalo to the offices of the law firm in which I was a fledgling attorney, not yet admitted to the bar. It was a Saturday, but in those ancient times Saturday was a normal workday. As I reached the big bank building in which the law firm occupied an upper floor, I realized that this was not a *normal* workday. A growing group of anxious people was assembling on the sidewalk outside the bank's ground-floor office. In the window was a big sign: "CLOSED." New York was one of twenty-two states in which all banks were closed by gubernatorial decree; two days later, the new president shut down every bank in the country.

We'd hit bottom. And with the knowledge that we had done so came a sense of release and a kind of wondering good cheer and togetherness in the face of disaster. The next day Will Rogers in his daily column reflected thus: "America hasn't been as happy in three years as they are today. No money, no banks, no work, no nothing." But he added that "the whole country is with him [Roosevelt]," exhibiting the astonishing degree of hope and confidence that Roosevelt's inaugural speech had inspired.

The president called a special session of Congress, which started by passing a measure providing for the reopening of the banks under a system of licensing and "conservators." This legislation—which was introduced, debated in both chambers, and enacted in one day, the first day of the special session— was the first of the "recovery" statutes of the New Deal. There were more to come, of course; even with the banking system saved for the moment, there were still the millions of unemployed and the millions of impoverished farmers. "Recovery" had to mean putting people back to work and giving the farmers a chance to make a living.

When I arrived in Washington in July 1933, for much of the country the New Deal was embodied by the National Recovery Administration, the NRA, established in June to administer the newly passed National Industrial Recovery Act. That statute also established a Public Works Administration, designed to put the unemployed to work on useful governmental projects. A month earlier Congress had passed the Federal Emergency Relief Act, authorizing massive grants to the states to provide sustenance and shelter for hungry or homeless millions. And for the farmers there was the Agricultural Adjustment Act: this, in effect, sought to lift farm prices by paying farmers to grow fewer crops and raise less livestock: hence the charge that Roosevelt and Secretary of Agriculture Wallace were "killing little pigs." The payments were financed by a tax on the processing of agricultural products.

There were others that I won't go into here (the Civilian Conservation Corps was one), but those four new programs were the basic "recovery" programs of the New Deal, designed to enable the country to survive a desperate emergency and to regain its economic health. The only one that I was directly concerned with was the NRA, under which each major industry, and some not so major, was supposed to establish a "code of fair competition." Industrialists were ready and willing to formulate and abide by codes that discouraged destructive, competitive price-slashing, imposed restrictions to prevent overproduction, established minimum wages, and even, in the case of the cotton industry, outlawed child labor. But many of them could not stomach Section 7a of the statute, which in effect compelled them to give their employees the right to bargain with them collectively through labor unions. The flouting of that provision led to great labor unrest and many strikes.

My agency, the Department of Labor, was of course concerned with these matters, and soon, as we shall see in the next
chapter, I was personally involved in settling some of those
strikes. Naturally, therefore, I soon became acquainted with
NRA officials who were trying to give effect to the labor provisions of the codes. I was also brought into occasional contact
with the extraordinary man whom Roosevelt had appointed to
head the NRA, General Hugh S. Johnson.

In the summer and early fall of 1933, for urban America
anyway, the NRA symbolized the New Deal itself, and Johnson
was its leader. "Old Ironpants," he was called, and he looked it,
with his creased visage, square jaw, and flushed (often, alas,
much too flushed) face. His voice was gravelly and his vocabu-
lary both vulgar and imaginative. To much of the public, I
think, his energy, force, and dramatic qualities made him seem
to be "Mr. New Deal" himself, in those early, heady days of
"reemployment agreements" and huge, noisy NRA parades
through cheering crowds. In one of those parades, General
Johnson and his young secretary and constant companion,
Frances "Robby" Robinson, rode in triumph, while the march-
ers sang. It was a familiar song and many knew its last two
lines: "Marching along together, Life is wonderful side by
side"; but now the words were "Marching along together,
Under the banner of NRA!"

Yet from the beginning Johnson's intemperance in behavior,
language, and thought was obvious and led inevitably to his
downfall. My own feelings about him were ambivalent. My letters often cast him in a devil's role. On September 8, 1933: "he
is trying to run *everything*. He's good—grand—only in his force
and persistence." Two weeks later: "Johnson cannot distinguish
between true and false." By the next spring I was calling him a
"public enemy . . . a pathological case [who] seeks to destroy all
who might thwart him and has no truth in him."

And yet—and yet! There was something marvelous about
him, and I knew it. Who else could have dreamed up the notion of plastering all the factories and store windows with a

patch of paper picturing the Blue Eagle, the sign of compliance with the NRA, and then growled to millions over the radio: "Don't trifle with that bird!" Who else could have told the Chicago Manufacturers Association that they were whirling dervishes beating tom-toms and throwing synthetic dead cats? And, granting that Roosevelt hated to fire anybody and therefore tended to be a bit vague in doing so, who but the general, after being told to take a different job, could have emerged from the Oval Office and said to waiting reporters: "I cannot leave. My feet are nailed to the floor!" I've always delighted in the inscription, on what is usually the dedication page, in his book *The Blue Eagle from Egg to Earth:* "Everybody here is a rinky-stink except Hughey Johnson, and he's all right:—Hugh S. Johnson, aged nine."

On March 15, 1934, when I was lunching at the Willard Hotel with Lincoln Filene (presumably to discuss unemployment insurance), we were joined by General Johnson and the ever-present "Robby" Robinson. Johnson took command of the conversation. I listened, listened carefully; and when I returned to my office, I promptly dictated all that I could remember of his monologue. Johnson speaking: "It's a crime to bring in a great industry to Washington and have it pilloried before the public here. The Labor Board has no right to make people come here anyway, and it has no power to enforce its order when it does make a finding. Every industry ought to police itself." At this point, presumably, he was speaking directly to me.

His next remarks reflected his own bitter disappointment in the president's decision, in June 1933, to split the recovery program established by the National Industrial Recovery Act into two parts: an NRA with its industry-wide codes under Johnson, and a Public Works Administration under Harold Ickes. The general had assumed that he would be in charge of both. At the Willard he continued: "If we had done things my way, we would have moved all these people from the places where industries are dying out onto three and a half acres of land apiece, putting them into cantonments: same idea as we had in the army. Then we would have had a million reemployed in October, in heavy industry caused by the construction of all those homes. That's what the planning in June should have been—but *somebody changed his mind.*"

Yes, things would have been very, very different if Johnson had had his way. For while the NRA moved almost too fast, with its "blanket code" covering businesses that were willing to comply with it while industry committees were still drafting enforceable codes for their own industries, the Public Works Administration seemed hardly to be moving at all. Harold Ickes, its director, was a combative, feisty man, and also a highly suspicious one. Not for nothing was he called "Honest Harold"; he was a longtime foe of corruption in city politics and was determined that there would be no corruption in the public works program.

While running that program he was also Secretary of the Interior. This slowed the public works effort further, for Ickes often seemed to think he had to do everything himself. He was especially fearful of delegating to subordinates the job of completing agreements with large building or highway contractors. In 1938 he moved into a brand-new Interior Department building, erected with PWA funds. His office in the old Interior building was then occupied by the president's "Uncle Fred," Frederick A. Delano, chairman of the National Resources Planning Board. Mr. Delano was amused to find, hidden on the underside of what had been Ickes's desk, a "bug" that recorded every conversation in that office. Honest Harold was seeing to it that he would never be accused of corruption and that no secret deals and corrupt side agreements would besmirch the public works program.

By the end of 1933, then, the PWA had put far fewer people to work than had been hoped. Two years later, however, thousands of projects had been approved and grants made to public agencies for the building of hospitals, sewer systems, streets, schools. Many of these "are still with us, . . . mute reminders of that brief moment in our history when the federal presence in American life was generally deemed more necessary than evil, and somewhere on most of these utilitarian monuments appear the words 'Harold L. Ickes, Secretary of the Interior. . . .' "* While the NRA had provided a prompt stimulus for at least a partial industrial recovery and a substantial amount of "reemployment," in the winter of 1933–34 there were still millions who couldn't work, or couldn't find work, and were in desperate need. For sustenance they had to depend on state largesse financed by the grants made by the FERA, the Federal Emergency Relief Administration.

The creation of this federal relief program was perhaps the most revolutionary act of the famous first hundred days of the New Deal. "Poor relief," as it was called, had always been assumed to be a task for state and local governments, not for the federal government. And even locally it was a task to be performed cautiously and sparingly, to help only the truly deserving poor who could not help themselves: the crippled, the aged, the hopelessly ill. Able-bodied people should go out and find a job; and even for the others, their plight was no concern of Washington. The fact that the Federal Emergency Relief Act did make it Washington's concern caused some bitter comments in the House of Representatives. For example, Representative Robert Luce of Massachusetts, whom we shall meet again later in this book, said, "It is socialism. Whether it is communism or not I do not know." Others saw it as "the end of our Federal system" of government. But these conservative voices went unheeded; so great was the need, so desperate the suffering, that the relief bill passed both houses by substantial margins.

Remember that in the early thirties there was no unemployment compensation, no Social Security, and, before 1933, hardly any money for outright relief—for "relief" was something that, according to Republican doctrine, the federal gov-

---

*T. H. Watkins, *Righteous Pilgrim* (New York: Henry Holt and Co., 1990), p. 373.

ernment must eschew, and the states were very nearly broke. Then came the New Deal. The ideological barrier was broken. Federal money was made available to succor the starving. And a lean, intense young Iowan, Harry Hopkins, was appointed to run the program. He was not concerned about the sanctity of the federal system, or the traditional reliance on private charity to aid the needy. He was just passionately intent on providing food for the hungry and shelter for the homeless.

Still, as Ronald Reagan liked to point out half a century later, Franklin Roosevelt, in his 1935 Annual Message to Congress, said that "The Federal government must and shall quit this business of relief." President Reagan, however, whether he knew it or not, was quoting the phrase grossly out of context. Roosevelt had continued: "It is a duty dictated by every intelligent consideration of national policy to ask you [the Congress] to make it possible for the United States to *give employment to all of these . . . people now on relief.* . . ."

Congress responded by establishing the Works Progress Administration, the WPA, and the unemployed were indeed put to work. This, too, was Harry Hopkins's agency, Harry Hopkins's program. I don't remember knowing any lawyers who worked for it. I'm sure that there weren't many. Harry Hopkins was not likely to surround himself with potential naysayers. I think that his desire—and ability—to help suffering people without worrying much about whether he had legal authority to do so was what especially attracted Roosevelt. The latter had a law degree but was never a notably successful practitioner, nor was he a stickler for legal niceties. He and Hopkins saw eye to eye on many things: Harry was a social worker by training, and F.D.R., as a perceptive columnist once wrote, was a "social worker at heart." Within a decade Hopkins had become the president's most intimate adviser as well as his emissary to our war-torn allies.

The WPA put millions of people to work. As Roosevelt was preparing to make the statement quoted above, he received a memorandum agreed to by both Hopkins of FERA and Ickes of PWA, urging that people be taken off the relief rolls and put to work on such things as highway construction and housing. Actually, soon after WPA came into existence, it provided for many other kinds of employment; unemployed actors found themselves treading the boards of WPA-sponsored theaters, musicians played in WPA orchestras, writers produced useful, readable histories of all the states of the Union.

Still, it was road construction that was the most visible of WPA projects and gave rise to frequent complaints that WPA workers weren't doing any work; they were just "leaning on their shovels." One day a very conservative lady in Cambridge, Massachusetts, saw them doing just that. She was approaching, on foot, the corner of Brattle Street and Sparks Street. Just beyond the corner there was in the road a large hole, and in front of it a towering pile of dirt. Between the lady and that pile stood five men, actually leaning on their shovels. The lady, advancing to the fray, demanded the attention of this idle group, asking, "Who's in charge here?" A large, smiling man of obvious Hibernian descent said: "Sure and I'm the foreman." "What do you mean," she snapped, "by just standing around doing nothing, in the middle of the morning?" He answered, "Come with me," and led her past the big pile of dirt. Then he pointed into the deep pit. There, six sweating men were vigorously digging. "This hole's got to be filled in when they finish," said the foreman, "but, ma'am, would ye have me bury them alive?"

For working and sometimes for loafing—I suppose there was some loafing—WPA workers received less than the normal wages for the types of employment involved. Federal budgetary restrictions—the federal deficit was mounting—kept their pay low. But what they did not receive in money was more than made up for by what they gained in self-respect. They had jobs: that was the important thing. And for the most part the jobs were on useful projects. Today, for instance, more than half a century later, in towns all across the country, schoolhouses built by the WPA are still standing and serviceable.

The fourth recovery program, as I've mentioned, was that of the Agricultural Adjustment Administration, the AAA. In today's urbanized America, when we speak of the unemployment rate during the Depression, too easily we forget that those figures relate to business and industry, not to farming. In fact, hard times came to the farms before they closed the factories. Agriculture was still a very important political interest, and the representatives and senators from the Midwest spoke forcefully for it. Their cause was aided by Franklin Roosevelt's choice of an innovative corn-grower and farm journal editor, Henry Agard Wallace, to be Secretary of Agriculture. Wallace, later Roosevelt's vice president (1941–45) and still later Harry Truman's independent opponent for the presidency in 1948, was a practical, even earthy, man when the subject he was dealing with was agriculture. Away from the soil, his personal insecurities and his imagination too often led him up strange, esoteric, even mystic, paths; he was a true idealist but not always a practical one.

I knew several of the AAA's young lawyers, including those two early housemates of mine, but aside from some involvement in a citrus-growers' strike I was never in official contact with the AAA. In 1935 my future wife and her younger sister, the latter dressed to the nines, did march in a parade of pickets outside the Agriculture building, protesting the administration's alleged injustice toward southern sharecroppers.

The essential parts of the statutes creating the NRA and the AAA were held unconstitutional by the Supreme Court. By the time the Court dealt this blow to the NRA, that agency was already in deep trouble. Johnson had finally departed; enforcement of code provisions had become ineffectual; there was mounting criticism that the whole program smacked of fascism, with big business taking over what was properly government's role. The decision did not abolish the NRA itself, but left it with nothing much to do. The large, mostly young, and very able staff of lawyers that had been extremely busy drafting industry codes and preparing the rules and regulations needed to enforce them was abruptly idled; I myself was able to put many of them back to work in a different agency within a few months of the Court decision.

The AAA decision was not so devastating. It was possible to devise a new statute that, in effect, continued the original program; and to this day, the government is still paying farmers for not growing crops.

Let us turn briefly to the New Deal statutes that were not primarily aimed at industrial, agricultural, or human "recovery" but at long-range "reform," the earliest objects of which were the banks and the stock market. We have seen how Congress acted swiftly to save the banking system; soon thereafter it provided for the deposit insurance that we know today. As for the stock market, the unregulated excesses of underwriters and brokers had been blamed—with good reason. However, the fault lay, too, in the get-rich-quick investing public for the great crash of 1929 and the Depression that followed it. "Never again" was the cry.

The first step was to ensure that the investing public be correctly informed about the corporations whose securities were offered for sale. In the autumn of 1933 somebody, probably Tom Corcoran at the behest of Felix Frankfurter, asked Professor James M. Landis of the Harvard Law School to come to Washington to draft a "Truth in Securities" bill. He did come, and for the two weeks before his family could join him he stayed at my first "bachelor house" on 18th Street.

Jim Landis was a brilliant, desperately intense, spare, hawk-faced man with a wide mouth that could resemble a cruel shark's mouth or be stretched into a winning smile. He seemed fated to become a figure in a Greek tragedy—and that's what happened, although prior to his final years of degradation (from income tax problems and alcohol) he had held, and done well in, many high and honorific positions, both private—dean of the Harvard Law School—and public—such as the chairmanship of the Federal Trade Commission, the Securities and Exchange Commission, and, much later, the Civil Aviation Board.

However, when he joined my housemates and me, such honors were all in the future. He expected to be treated as an equal; he had been our teacher (he was a fine teacher) but he was only a few years older than we were. He worked intensely on his drafting job, and before the fortnight was over was very tired and consequently pretty glum. I felt sympathetic; I not only respected his dedication to his task, but I liked him very much. But his gloomy silence and occasional irritable outbursts annoyed at least one of my housemates; I remember my horror when Frank Shea proposed, gleefully, that we "toss Jim Landis in a blanket."

He had hardly left us before Telford Taylor, as I have mentioned, began to help draft a much more far-reaching and controversial bill than the "Truth in Securities" Act. It was a true reform measure, designed to prevent any recurrence of the stock market debacle of 1929—to rein in the speculative forces that led to that disaster. Now it may well be true, as John Kenneth Galbraith has pointed out,* that financial panics are caused not by technical flaws in the free market process but by the speculative mania that seizes the public every few decades; but in 1933–35 it was considered imperative to regulate the stock exchanges more firmly and reduce the temptation to gamble by buying shares "on margin." Thousands of investors had lost everything. They bought shares on credit—hardly any cash down—counting on the value of those stocks to rise, and were still holding them when the market collapsed. Hence the enactment of the Securities and Exchange Act of 1935, and who can say positively that its restrictive provisions did not discourage, if not prevent, a speculative stock-buying orgy for the next forty-five years?

The Securities and Exchange Act, in my view the first of the major "reform statutes" of the New Deal, became law in June 1934. The other laws of lasting importance that could be given the same title were enacted a year later. They were the National Labor Relations Act, drastically changing the relationship of

*J. K. Galbraith, *A Short History of Financial Euphoria* (Nashville: Whittle Direct Books, 1990).

employers and employees, and the Social Security Act, committing the federal government to participation in the task of succoring the needy, and also providing insurance against the vicissitudes of unemployment and old age. These we will consider in ensuing chapters.

Although I have categorized some New Deal measures as "recovery" and some "reform," it appears that a different dichotomy has been perceived by historians, and was, indeed, the subject of considerable argument in Washington. Arthur M. Schlesinger, Jr., for example, made what he called the change from a "first" New Deal to a "second" New Deal the conceptual framework of the third volume of his "Age of Roosevelt" series. My difficulties with this notion that there were a "first" and "second" New Deal are caused, I suppose, by my own pragmatic, non-ideological attitude, as well as by the fact that I took no part in the intellectual battle that apparently was going on to obtain the president's ear and to guide him along preferred paths of policy. Fortunately, Roosevelt, too, was a pragmatist, neither ideological nor intellectual: I'm sure that if he'd been told that there had been two New Deals he would just have said, genially, "That's an idea," and let it go at that.

As to the dispute itself: on one side were the people who believed in centralized national direction of the economy, even if this meant an enlargement of corporate power through instruments such as the NRA; on the other, the decentralizers who, distrustful of big business (and some of them, also, of big government), would leave much decision making to the states. Financier Bernard Baruch, sitting on a bench in Lafayette Park, was said to be the *eminence grise* of the first group, with Rexford Tugwell as his front man,* and Justice Brandeis supposedly inspired the second faction.

The first, Tugwellian, period, typified by the National Industrial Recovery Act, ended in May 1935, when the Supreme

---

*"The New Deal of 1933 had rested on a faith in centralized coordination. . . . In the crisis of 1933, men from Tugwell on the left to Baruch on the right subordinated their differences to work together in that common faith." (A. M. Schlesinger, Jr., *The Politics of Upheaval* [Boston: Houghton Mifflin, 1960] p. 212). The combination of Tugwell and Baruch was indeed odd.

Court struck down that statute. Then came the Second New Deal, dominated by the Brandeisian notion that small is beautiful. However, although Professor Schlesinger had written a magnificent account of the early days, *The Coming of the New Deal,* in this later volume his conceptual framework really did not fit the facts. Take the Social Security Act, for instance: enacted in August 1935, it was both Tugwellian and Brandeisian—a New Deal measure, but not a "first" or "second" New Deal measure. Old age insurance was centralized, unemployment insurance and public welfare decentralized (with, admittedly, a federal prod).

I assume that this ideological struggle was indeed going on. After all, it had deep historic roots, going back to Thomas Jefferson's fundamental disagreement with Alexander Hamilton. In our own century, just before the First World War the Progressive movement was riven by the opposition of many reformers to the belief, advocated by many others, that the nation's economic life should be controlled jointly by the federal government and big business. So in the thirties a similar clash of opinions was not surprising; but I doubt that Franklin Roosevelt thought that he had to make a choice between the two views. Yes, he listened to Tugwell, then Assistant Secretary of Agriculture, who was a member of his "Brains Trust," and also to "Isaiah," as he privately called Brandeis. But he did not commit himself to either side.

As for me, I was never involved in this ideological conflict, and only dimly aware of it. I did get a glimmering of its existence when Tugwell stimulated Roosevelt's interest in unemployment insurance by telling him, mistakenly, that the states' unemployment reserve funds, if turned over to the federal government, would just about eliminate the need for federal borrowing and thus solve the "currency problem." And one of my occasional evenings at the Jouett Shouses' was spent "discussing nationalization." But I cannot recall hearing a word about the subject from any of my housemates, or from any other young lawyers.

What I do recall, of course, is the sense of participation in a peaceful revolution. Few of the young New Dealers shared the determination of Tugwell, expressed in a poem written in his student days, to "roll up my sleeves and make America over"; but we did know that only great conceptual and practical changes could save the country from chaos, and we felt that it was our job to help to formulate those practical changes and to make them work. In my own case, my attention was focused, first, on ways to achieve a just industrial peace, and, second, on the need for social insurance; and these concerns are the subject of the next chapters of this book.

Chapter 3

Labor

————

Iᴛ ᴡᴀs just by chance that I joined the Labor Department rather than some other agency of the government such as the National Recovery Administration (the NRA), which was hiring a considerable number of young lawyers. In my boyhood, labor unions were mentioned seldom, and never favorably. My grandfather, it was reported—I can't find the citation—had said that "the scab is an American hero." My father denounced union rules that made a craftsman lay down his tools at five o'clock when he could have finished the job in fifteen minutes more. My brother, like many other Harvard students, had volunteered for police duty during the Boston policemen's strike of 1919.

Eventually, however, my eldest sister, Rosamond, expressed views more sympathetic to the "working stiff"; she was in training to become a social worker. And at law school, any anti-labor prejudice that I may have had disappeared. In the constitutional law course, I found myself wholeheartedly agreeing with Holmes and Brandeis when they dissented from opinions that, for example, held that states could not outlaw "yellow-dog contracts"—those that let an employer say, "You can have the job if you promise not to join a union"; and I was keenly interested in Jim Landis's course on labor law. Only a few students took that course, for to most of us, even as late as 1932, "labor law" seemed to be an esoteric and irrelevant subject.

In the late spring of 1933, when I was practicing law in Buffalo, I read that Charles Wyzanski had been named Solicitor of the Labor Department. This roused my hope of getting to Washington myself: just to Washington and into the New Deal, not particularly into that department, though I did like what I had heard about the new Secretary of Labor, Frances Perkins. My acquaintance with Wyzanski at that time being friendly but not intimate, I wrote to a mutual friend in Boston, Alexander Hawes, saying that I was enthusiastic about Charlie's appointment and would greatly enjoy working for him. This devious approach worked. Wyzanski had not yet left Boston. Hawes told him about my letter. And on arriving in Washington, Wyzanski invited me to join his staff.

For some arcane reason, the Solicitor's Office was then under the jurisdiction of the Justice Department. That meant my appointment required the approval of the attorney-general, and *that*, in turn, usually needed the acquiescence of James A. Farley, postmaster general and chairman of the Democratic National Committee. Fortunately this caused no trouble, even though I hadn't been FRBC ("for Roosevelt before Chicago"). I'd sentimentally favored the nomination of Al Smith, and as a practical matter favored and expected the nomination of Newton D. Baker.* But after F.D.R. won at the Chicago convention I was all for him and was welcomed gladly by the Buffalo Democratic City Committee when I volunteered my oratorical talents, minimal though they were. I made numerous speeches during the campaign, including one from the flatbed of a truck, at lunch hour, right outside the offices of the law firm that employed me. As most of the firm's partners despised Roosevelt, this took a little nerve, but I took courage from the fact that a founding member of the firm had been a Democratic president, Grover Cleveland. The endorsement of the party's City Committee smoothed my way into the Labor Department.

I was the first lawyer appointed by Wyzanski, who had in-

---

*At Harvard's Democratic "mock convention," over which I presided in 1932, a deadlock between Roosevelt and Smith was broken by the nomination of Baker. At the real convention two months later, the same thing very nearly happened. The Roosevelt forces averted it, after three inconclusive ballots, by inducing John N. Garner to swing his votes to F.D.R., and there were just enough of these to secure the nomination for Roosevelt.

herited three others, one of whom was about to leave. The remaining two were pleasant, middle-aged men who apparently had spent many years in the unexciting task of checking the validity and sufficiency of immigration bonds. They were amiable gentlemen. One of them liked to relieve the tedium by telling amusing stories. Late one afternoon he was in the middle of a story when he glanced up, saw that it was five o'clock, stopped talking, rose, and departed. It wasn't only union men who downed tools at the appointed hour!

In the final two years of the Hoover administration, the Labor Department had fallen into not-so-innocuous desuetude. The figures produced by its Bureau of Labor Statistics were unreliable or, to be frank about it, false; indeed, Miss Perkins's reputation was high, nationally, because as Industrial Commissioner in New York she had exposed their falsity. More than three-quarters of the department's annual budget had gone to the Immigration and Naturalization Service, which was not only mismanaged, under Secretary W. N. Doak, but decidedly corrupt. George Martin, in his splendid biography of Miss Perkins entitled *Madam Secretary*, has told of how she confronted a group of very tough Immigration inspectors whose jobs had been discontinued; they were rifling the files, and would undoubtedly have shredded them if there had been shredders in those days. She courageously ordered them to leave. After a few tense moments they did leave. But—and this is not in Martin's book—she was sure that they would seek revenge; there were indeed indications that someone once planted fake incriminating documents in the desk of the Secretary herself. She had taken office in March; four months later there was still concern about what Murray Garson, who had headed the worst of the Immigration enforcement divisions, and his merry men might do.

I had been at work for only a couple of days when I asked Wyzanski: "Who's Mr. Martin?" (No relation of George Martin!) "I keep meeting him in the hall on the seventh floor, outside the Secretary's office, and he's very pleasant, but I can't see that he does anything. What *does* he do?" "Oh," said Charlie vaguely, "I guess he's got something to do with the Conciliation Service." "He doesn't look like a conciliator to me; he looks like a private detective." Charlie laughed and said: "Yes, he is, but he must be a pretty poor detective if you've spotted him so quickly!"

The Conciliation Service, an agency for preventing or settling strikes through mediation, was one of the reasonably respectable branches of the department that Miss Perkins inherited. The others were the Children's Bureau and the Women's Bureau, with which I never had much contact. I did have a great deal of contact with the Conciliation Service. I liked the gentle head of the service, Hugh Kerwin ("Mr. Chips," Charlie called him), and came to have a very friendly acquaintance with several of his men, for within a few weeks I myself was involved in strike settling. That, however, came later; my first assignment was to prepare an answer to an indignant letter from a lady in Idaho. She had written to the Secretary demanding to know what right the latter had to call herself "Miss Perkins" when she was actually Mrs. Paul Wilson. The writer wanted to use her maiden name, too, but she couldn't. I actually looked up some law, including that of Idaho, before assuring her that she could call herself whatever she liked.

Although at the department I seldom "looked up law" (which is what I'd been doing for a year in Buffalo) I did do some of that, as shown by my first letter home after arriving in Washington: "The first three days in the office have been decidedly interesting. . . . Charlie took me around the department, introducing me to various people. The Secretary reminded me a little of 'Aunt Hat.' [Harriot Curtis, my cousins' aunt.] It seems that the President appointed the Sec'y of State, the Sec'y of Labor, and the Attorney-General a committee to codify and improve the nationality laws, whatever they are, and that's my job. It is almost like taking a first year course at law school, for the work now consists of studying statutes, cases, and memoranda. There are other things at intervals:

yesterday I had the pleasure of formulating the Department's attitude toward proposed *municipal* minimum wage ordinances, over Miss Perkins' signature."

Two weeks later: "I'm going to be responsible for a legislative service for the Department, keeping track of bills and hearings and arranging for the appropriate people to testify." Already I was straying from ordinary legal work. And in August 1933 I found myself immersed in labor relations. "I got a break when Charlie said that the National Labor Board had decided to co-operate with the Labor Dept. and I was to be the liaison officer. This was partly because Friday p.m. I had grabbed a chance to handle a telegram from Mississippi about threats of lynching strikers there, and had satisfied the Board's secretary with my (Miss Perkins's) reply. The secretary of the NLB, whom I consult daily, is one Dr. William M. Leiserson, a very sunny little man from the Antioch faculty. All this week my desk has been flooded with letters and telegrams to the Secretary of Labor about strikes, labor disputes, and violations of the NRA. Some I answer, some send direct to the NLB, some take to discuss with Leiserson. He has a similar pile and I bring back some of it for our conciliation service."

As this last letter suggests, labor unrest was rapidly spreading and strikes multiplying. Why? Having become an instant expert on the subject, I decided to share my wisdom with the public. I dashed off a long article that appeared in the Boston *Sunday Globe* in early September 1933, filling a whole page. Some of it I will quote here. The style is a bit oratorical, as if I were making a campaign speech, but it does do a pretty good job of explaining the situation and of describing the efforts to deal with it; also, incidentally, it expresses my own viewpoint and reflects my own feeling of excitement and enthusiasm.

> During the years of depression, much ground that had been gained by organized labor was lost. In unions, numbers is strength, and since 1929 the numerical strength of trade unions in America has fallen off tremendously. This was due largely to fairly obvious reasons: with so many men unemployed, others

feared to strike lest they permanently lost their jobs, and with wages down to almost nothing those who had jobs could not afford to pay union dues.

But now there is a change. The workers feel that the tide has turned. They feel—and with good reason—that in the new spirit that lies behind this great experiment of partnership between the industry of the individual and the Government of all the people they are presented with the greatest opportunity in the history of industrial labor.

For they have been taken into that partnership. Spurred on by the ever-increasing number of jobs that are opening up, stimulated by the explicit recognition of the right to collective bargaining in the National Industrial Recovery Act, labor is organizing as never before. . . . But why the strikes? Partly, of course, because the strike is the most effective weapon of unionizing a non-union shop, where the employer is not ready to recognize a union. Many of the strikes that are going on at present are simply battles for recognition. And where that is the sole issue, labor must be the winner. The Recovery Act, in Section 7a, gives the workers the right to collective bargaining through representatives of their own choosing. . . .

Turning to the codes promulgated by the NRA for each major industry, which included provisions prescribing minimum wages, I wrote that these "create a condition where disputes are almost inevitable and it is hard to take sides. Rightly or wrongly, skilled laborers, men who have learned a trade, are apt to feel that they are on a different social scale from the unskilled laborer. For years they have been getting wages double those of the common laborer. But now what happens? Six months ago the skilled mechanic in a plant was getting, say, 43 cents an hour, and the unskilled fellow . . . 21 cents an hour. Now comes the Code, with a minimum wage of 40 cents. The employer boosts his unskilled men to that figure and then, naturally, says that he cannot afford to raise anyone else's pay." To this cause of discontent and strikes, I could suggest no solution except "the give-and-take of bargaining between the craftsman and the operator."

Thus far, my article suggested that its author had a strong pro-labor bias. But in ensuing paragraphs I mentioned interunion struggles as a further cause of strife. John L. Lewis and his "industrial unions" had not yet established the C.I.O., but the battle lines were forming, and the old-time craft unions of the American Federation of Labor were on the defensive. And I did show that I had at least a glimmer of understanding of how the employers felt:

> Not unnaturally, employers who have long operated their business with non-union men resent the arrival of union organizers on the scene. Quite understandably, union leaders long in the saddle will fight, rather than be unhorsed by a new leader of a rebel crew. But . . . the United States Government stands ready to pacify the combatants before the gun-play stage or, if possible, even before the walkout.
>
> In the Department of Labor is the United States Conciliation Service, with a staff of 27 men scattered over the country, ready to hasten to the scene of conflict and offer mediation. Director Hugh L. Kerwin, in Washington, is busy these days. The telephone rings; long-distance, Utica calling; strike in hat factory called for tomorrow. Off goes a telegram to the conciliator in Buffalo: "Proceed Utica." The conciliator, striving to stop a walkout on the lakefront, entrains for Utica, talks with the owner and the union head, proposes a settlement, sees the strike called off. Then he goes back to Buffalo where both sides, in embattled mood, reject his suggestions. Then another telegram, and he is off to Cleveland to see if he can keep the stonecutters there at work and satisfied. That done, he resumes his efforts among the Buffalo longshoremen.
>
> The Conciliation Service cannot carry a big stick. . . . It is just an agency that is always ready to act as peacemaker, on the principle that the whole people has an interest in the prevention or settlement of industrial disputes upon just terms.

Section 7a of the National Industrial Recovery Act, however, needed to be enforced; only three months old, it was already being defied by employers all over the country. Enforcement would require a bigger stick than the Labor Department possessed. Furthermore, any use of a big stick could have had a disastrous effect on the whole NRA program, for the acquiescence of industry to code provisions boosting wages would be hard to obtain from defiant non-union employers.

The Conciliation Service was too small. It did not have enough influence. (Incidentally, I didn't know it existed until I went to Washington!) What was needed was a super-conciliation body that could at least tell the warring parties what to do, even though it couldn't make them do it. Accordingly, a National Labor Board was established within the NRA, headed by Senator Robert F. Wagner of New York and otherwise composed of nationally known leaders of industry and labor. It was with this board that I "liaised," to use a recent neologism, on behalf of the Secretary of Labor and the Conciliation Service.

My *Globe* article described this board and its functions, but perhaps more graphic and certainly less restrained were my exuberantly juvenile letters about it. On August 11, 1933:

> Yesterday I had a tremendously interesting time attending the first real meeting of the National Labor Board. They settled a two-months strike in Reading, Pa. (15,000 men), in 3 hours. There were several union men there, and several rather passionate employers, their spokesman a very Prussian gentleman who had no desire to let the workers vote to unionize. (He was particularly sore because when the strikers, parading, passed his house they all goose-stepped!) There was a good deal of backing and filling, the Board consulting with itself, with the employers alone, and with both sides, and finally the employers going into a huddle and giving in.
>
> Gerard Swope of General Electric was marvelous. In looks and manner he reminded me of Frank Moulan, the Lord Chancellor in the Winthrop Ames production of *Iolanthe*—and also of George Arliss as Disraeli because of his tact and his dramatic quality, acting every instant and in complete control. His prestige is so great that I expect they will let him do most of the handling of the employers.
>
> I talked outside with [two board members,] Mr. Kirstein of Filene's and Walter Teagle of Standard Oil, a huge and surprisingly genial soul with an odd habit of laughing silently at his own thoughts. The two labor representatives on the Board are pretty awful. John L. Lewis is a dishonest thug, but Kirstein thinks he's less harmful on the Board than off. William Green, President of the A. F. of L., is amiable enough, but is forever making great orations on extraneous matters. He nearly upset the applecart

yesterday by launching into one of these just when Swope had gained the first real concession from the employers.

(Here, in fairness to myself, I should pause long enough to modify, or rather expand upon, my description of John L. Lewis. He was of course much more than a "dishonest thug." I never knew him well, but I came to have a good deal of respect for his brains and his rough, tough, leadership qualities. And I was always amused by his habit, when about to take a seat, of turning the chair around and sitting on it astride, as though he were riding a horse.)

Now we return briefly to the conclusion of my *Globe* article—or oration (as thousands cheer). After describing how the board—specifically Wagner in one case, Teagle in another—settled several strikes, I wrote:

> Two men the American people will look upon without a drop of sympathy. One is the labor agitator who seeks only personal power, or who prefers violence to peaceful negotiation. The other is the employer who is ready to flout the law in his endeavor to keep the old order intact. For the old order changeth. We are developing a system wherein the irrepressible conflict has no place.... We are all in the same boat. The cause of our troubles is the maldistribution of the world's goods. We seek a more equable distribution. It is a course upon which all alike agree—workers, employers, and the people's government.... The workers of the country must be given not only a new deal but a square deal. The American people is in truth making a supreme effort to save and to improve our national existence.

I quote these phrases here because their very hyperbole evokes memories of how things were in the summer of 1933: the sense of mortal peril and immortal hope.

At the same time that I was writing that article I was trying to promote a plan to expand the department's influence by having the NRA, which was amply funded, pay for a major increase in the Conciliation Service. I sold this idea to Ed McGrady, Assistant Secretary of Labor. It was a good idea; the National Labor Board would handle only a tiny percentage of labor disputes, and the various "Code Authorities" that were being established were most unlikely mediators. Miss Perkins could probably have persuaded Wagner to support this notion. She did not try to, for at least two reasons. First, she herself really had no keen interest in labor disputes and strikes; and second, even she and Wagner together would have had little chance of getting General Johnson, administrator of the NRA, to agree to this plan. So the department's Conciliation Service remained shorthanded. Not quite consciously, I found this to be an opportunity for myself. I liked Mr. Kerwin of the Conciliation Service, and he apparently liked me. Before long I was directly involved, sporadically but enthusiastically, in strike settling.

As early as September 15, 1933, I was writing home exultantly: "Hooray! The Camden dispute is settled—they all agree—I was peaches and cream to both sides and sent soft soap shooting over the telephone wires." In a letter to Richard Berresford I was more specific: "I did my first strike-settling the other day, largely by long-distance telephone. RCA Victor in Camden, N.J., had fired a guy who was organizing a union. He came down—sent by the union—in an awful sweat and later sent me tragic telegrams about his wife and kiddies. I finally got them (employer and employees, not wife and kiddies) to stop scrapping and he went back to a job in the plant paying $2 a week more than he'd been getting before."

While I was all for upholding the workers' rights under Section 7a, and highly critical of employers who denied them those rights, I was not automatically pro-union. Far from it. Frequently I wrote scornfully about the leaders of some of the major A.F. of L. craft unions, especially in the building trades, calling them "a bunch of racketeers in league with a lot of the building contractors." And again: "It's hard to be enthusiastic about organized labor." Those were early comments, but in 1934 I still felt the same way: "I'd like to see equality of bargaining power, but I doubt the efficacy of any program designed to increase the strength of the A.F. of L. as at present constituted. There is a dearth of disinterested labor leaders. If some of the top men could be deported, and Sidney Hillman and Philip Murray and a few men like that put in charge, then we'd have a worth-while labor movement." I did not guess that I was anticipating F.D.R.'s famous remark, a few years later, that so infuriated John L. Lewis: "A plague on both your houses!"

My overstated skepticism was a good thing; conciliators are supposed to be impartial. Not all of the New Dealers were impartial. I'm reminded of the embarrassment of Lloyd K. Garrison, the fine chairman of the National Labor Relations Board that briefly succeeded the original National Labor Board and functioned until the passage of the National Labor Relations Act in June 1935. Garrison was trying to persuade Richard Harte, a shovel manufacturer in West Virginia, to permit his employees to vote on whether they wanted a union and, if so, which union, to represent them. The election would be run by the NLRB; and the NLRB, Garrison assured Harte, was absolutely impartial. Harte said he would think it over. As the two men stepped out of the chairman's office, a door down the hall was flung open. From it emerged Estelle Frankfurter, sister of Felix Frankfurter and an NLRB employee. "Lloyd, Lloyd!" she cried. "You know about that election at that plant in Cincinnati? We won! We won!"

Well, I was less biased (and more discreet, except when writing letters!) than she was, but I must have had an awful lot of chutzpah. A diary entry early in 1934 reads: "Consulted with Mr. Kerwin as to Labor Department's intervention in aluminum strike in New Kensington, Pa.; advised Kerwin to go ahead and send Mr. Colvin there." Advised Kerwin? Did I think I was running the U.S. Conciliation Service? But I'm sure Kerwin did not resent it; he knew that he needed all the help he could get. Later that spring, perhaps because both Miss Perkins and Wyzanski were absent for a while, I got deeply involved in the handling of a couple of major disputes.

One of these was in Toledo, Ohio. The department had Conciliator Dunnigan on the scene, but the key figure in the strike-settling effort was Charles P. Taft, son of President Taft. Just what his official position was, I do not recall. "That was a rather small strike," I wrote on May 27, 1934:

> but three weeks ago the police force was cut down from 350 to 50, and the beginning of violence toward the strikebreakers was the signal for all the hoodlums to start throwing bricks through windows, reminiscent of the Boston police strike. Then as the company's attitude was shown to be arbitrary and high-handed, genuine labor sympathizers joined in. Now, however, truckloads of communists are arriving and the strikers suddenly took a position as arbitrary as that of the company, so Taft has a tough job. . . . Ah—telephone from Taft in Toledo. The employers changed their attitude and promptly the labor attitude changed too. He hopes for a complete settlement tomorrow. I do hope he's right.

From that day until June 7, all the top officials of the department—the Secretary, the Assistant Secretary, the Assistant to the Secretary, and the Solicitor—were out of town, so I was not only Acting Solicitor but, as I claimed in a note to Berresford, "unofficial acting Secretary," aged twenty-six. My diary for that period, dictated and therefore much more prudently worded than my letters, included this paragraph: "Toledo—kept in communication with Charles P. Taft and Dunnigan until the strikes there were settled. Received a telephone call from Governor White of Ohio. Also one from Congressman Duffy of Toledo, who abused the Secretary, made a number of very strange statements, and said he was going to issue a public denunciation of the Department. Checked up on him and heard soon from Judge Florence Allen that he carried no weight and was a drunk, which was obvious."

Camden, New Jersey, came into the picture again that spring, this time concerning a strike at the New York Shipbuilding Company's shipyards there. The situation was absurdly complicated. The Navy Department was involved, for naval vessels were being built in Camden. Public Works Administration funds were helping to pay for them. The NRA was doubly interested, for it had not only a Shipbuilders' Code

Industrial Relations Board, but a Regional Labor Board based in Newark. And because our department was, after all, the Department of Labor, the press and the public assumed that ours was the responsibility for settling the strike.

On April 8, my diary reported that "J. David Stern, owner of the New York *Evening Post,* asked what we were going to do about the shipbuilding strike at Camden. I told Kerwin to send (conciliator) Chappell, and got him to inform Wharton of the Shipbuilders' Code Industrial Relations Board, which he did with great reluctance; told Winship, deputy administrator of the NRA, and the National Labor Board of the action we were taking regardless of the notion that the Code Board was supposed to have charge of the case. Telephoned Mr. Stern to tell him we were taking this action." Talk about being high-handed!

The agencies that I so summarily swept aside, or tried to sweep aside, did not go gently. A few days later, I "talked with Chappell about the shipbuilding strike, and dictated a memorandum pointing our jurisdictional conflict between this Department, Regional Labor Board, and Code Industrial Relations Board." Meanwhile, the strike dragged on. On the same day, I "met with the Secretary and a delegation of 26 strikers from Camden; heard their complaints; investigated the legality of the ship-building contracts which their company had [with the navy], calling at the office of Lieutenant Commander Pennoyer; investigated and agreed with the claim that PWA wage rates should apply, calling Mr. Hunt, General Counsel of the PWA; advised Chappell to urge compromise; and took part in Secretary's endeavor to send them away not too dissatisfied."

On April 20, Jesse Miller of the National Labor Board staff agreed to call off the Newark Board from the shipyard case. Three days later, I met with the "Code Board" and they agreed to keep their hands off. I "telegraphed Chappell to continue as sole Government representative in the Camden shipbuilding strike." However, by this time there was one other individual who had decided that *he* would settle the strike: namely, Hugh S. Johnson, administrator of the NRA.

I met with General Johnson and Ed McGrady, Assistant Secretary of Labor, on May 3, armed with a supposedly conciliatory suggestion by Miss Perkins, that she and Secretary of Commerce Daniel C. Roper appoint three new members to the Code Board (one of whom would be me), and count on that enlarged board to settle the strike. Johnson was scornful: "She obviously misunderstands the whole idea of the NRA," he said. When McGrady and I made it clear to him that Bardo (president of New York Shipbuilding Company) was paying wages lower than other shipyards, Johnson declared: "I'll settle this. I'll call that bastard in here and teach him to be a good citizen."

The general did call Bardo in, but taught him nothing; on May 4, "Chappell reported that Johnson had seen Bardo and failed to make any impression on him whatever." Then Johnson called another conference, inviting not only Bardo but the employer members of the Code Board and some union representatives. He ended up by saying that he would make an "investigation," a delaying tactic harmful to the strikers.

Ed McGrady and I attended that conference. We stayed, as did Johnson and Bardo, after the others had left, and discussed the workers' demand for a 15 percent wage increase. Bardo said that he could not go above 13 percent "or it would break him." I remarked that he had earlier said the same thing about going above 10 percent, yet now he was willing to raise wages 13 percent. Bardo growled, "I wasn't born yesterday," got up, and left. McGrady and I then went into an adjoining room where the union men were waiting. Dramatically, McGrady cried; "Boys, the fight is on!"*—but I skeptically re-

---

*This was not the only time that Ed McGrady startled and amused me. Once, as an unofficial conciliator, I was sitting with him to hear the complaints of the imposing, immensely wealthy president of the Great Atlantic & Pacific Tea Company, G. Huntington Hartford. Speaking very softly and sadly, Mr. Hartford said: "The trouble began. Our fair city fell ill. Our mayor did nothing. The illness grew worse. The city suffered." (McGrady closed his eyes, but Hartford did not raise his voice.) "Our people suffered. And still our mayor did nothing. And now the illness bids fair to become fatal, and our city, once one of the finest, . . ."

McGrady opened his eyes and shouted: "Cut out the horseshit!" Hartford did not bat an eye. Very quietly he said: "You don't know our mayor, Mr. McGrady. He is one revolting son of a bitch."

marked in my diary: "Just what good that will do them I don't know."

My skepticism was not justified. Himself an old union officer, Ed McGrady knew how to raise the spirits of the rank and file. Five days later, the strike ended in what I called a "virtual victory" for the strikers, with Conciliator Chappell the only government man involved in the final settlement process. Soon I was writing home: "One thing we were successful at. The patience of our Labor Dept. conciliator, Miss Perkins' insistence, my endeavors to get the Public Works Administration interested in naval construction wages, and above all the intelligence of the strikers finally resulted in a satisfactory settlement of the shipyard strike in Camden, after General Johnson had failed so completely to influence the employer." Next day, as I wrote home, Miss Perkins and the general were at the White House. "Said Johnson: 'Oh, by the way, Mr. President, I got that Camden strike settled all right.' Miss Perkins said she nearly—but not quite—got up and *screamed!*"

Later that month, after it was falsely rumored in the press that Miss Perkins would resign, I wrote home: "They (some newspaper columnists) talk more tripe! The real funny occurrence, though, came as a result of that story. Miss Perkins yesterday received a friendly call from a man who said he just dropped in to cheer her up, that she was not to worry about this 'sniping.' The snipers weren't worth a nickel and she must not mind being sniped at. The caller was our old buddy General Johnson."

Although his days in office were numbered, the general was still around when the biggest labor disputes in which I was involved took place in the early summer of 1934. These were the strikes of longshoremen and seafaring personnel that tied up all shipping on the Pacific Coast. In June, after scuttling the Wagner Labor Disputes bill, Roosevelt had virtually dictated Public Resolution 44, authorizing him, in cooperation with the Department of Labor, to appoint special boards to deal with specific disputes. The first such board to be appointed was the three-member National Longshoremen's Board, based in San

Francisco. On July 18 I was sent out there to assist the board, returning after a couple of very busy weeks. There was little time for letter writing, but after my return I prepared a lengthy, detailed report for Secretary Perkins, a copy of which refreshes my memory today.

Actually, I arrived in San Francisco just after the excitement and the sense of crisis had reached its peak. The longshoremen had been on strike for two months, the seamen for several weeks; the sympathetic three-day work stoppage of all the unions in San Francisco had just ended. The violence that helped Harry Bridges to bring about that stoppage, when police used force in helping strikebreakers to transport goods from the waterfront, had occurred two weeks before. It had been followed by almost hysterical pleas from San Francisco business leaders, that the president "do something" to save the city.

The president was vacationing at sea, far out on the Pacific. Miss Perkins steadfastly refused to urge him to return. The National Longshoremen's Board would handle everything. As usual, her attitude was that a strike was a strike and so what? A San Francisco newspaper really took out after her when it learned that shipowner and former Mayor Roger Lapham, whom she had known for many years, had telephoned her (at two in the morning, eastern time), and she had said: "Oh, stop behaving like a three-year-old child, Roger!" In her persistent refusal she had, so I claimed in a later letter, followed the advice of "O. K. Cushing, Ed McGrady, Charlie and me," but I doubt if any such advice was needed except possibly that of O. K. Cushing.

Mr. Cushing was a member of the National Longshoremen's Board. So was Ed McGrady. The chairman of the board was the Roman Catholic archbishop of San Francisco, Edward J. Hanna. Cushing, a successful lawyer, had been prominent in the life of his city for thirty years—had, indeed, headed the relief effort there after the great earthquake and fire of 1906. The Secretary felt, correctly, that he understood the whole situation, and even if she didn't need his advice she was glad that it confirmed her own opinion. With McGrady she was less at ease, and vice versa; my diary entries suggest that he seldom called *her*, for almost every day before I left for the Coast I noted, "Telephone call [to me] from Ed McGrady." As far as I know, she had no communication at all with Archbishop Hanna.

When I arrived in San Francisco the so-called general strike was over and the city appeared normal, except for some National Guards on the waterfront and a large number of steamers anchored in the harbor. Three of the latter were called "housing ships" because they housed idle strikebreakers. There was still plenty of tension evident, however. The Hearst paper and the *Chronicle* were by now suggesting that the strikes of the longshoremen and seamen were "Communist-inspired." And by bad luck, Hugh S. Johnson, on a speaking tour to tout the NRA, had made a long-scheduled speech at the University of California on the second day of the general work stoppage, which he called "this ugly thing . . . a blow at the flag of our common country." He continued: "If the Federal Government did not act, this people would act, and it would act to wipe out this subversive element as you clean off a chalk mark on a blackboard with a wet sponge."

As an invitation to "this people" to take the law into their own hands, this was effective: promptly, vigilante committees were formed in San Francisco and other California cities, and people suspected of "communist leanings" were beaten up. So it was a relief, when I met McGrady that first morning, to learn that the general was about to leave town. McGrady would fly with him to Los Angeles. I spoke with Johnson before they departed, and to my amazement the general urged me to accompany them. For the first time, I became aware of Johnson's impending crack-up; as early as noontime, he was just plain drunk.

Of course I stayed in San Francisco, and on the following morning did something really useful. James A. Farley had arrived to make a speech to the Commonwealth Club. As I later reported to Miss Perkins, "I went to see the Postmaster General at his hotel. Mr. Farley received me very warmly and showed me two paragraphs which he had been intending to use in his speech. They related to the strike, quoting some of General Johnson's most tactless remarks, and dwelt on 'loyal citizens' and 'subversive agitators.' He asked me if I approved of them and I said that I did not. He then asked me to write a paragraph in place of them. I did so, having him congratulate San Francisco on using cool common sense and making a number of other highly innocuous remarks. He took it verbatim."

Just why I went to see Farley I don't recall—probably Mr. Cushing, fearing another inflammatory speech, had told me to do so. Nor do I recall why Senator Wagner was on the Coast at that time. He met with the board that weekend (as did I), when the central question was whether to submit the disputes to binding arbitration. The longshoremen's leaders in Portland, Oregon, had already been persuaded by Wagner that this was the wisest course; now their leaders in San Francisco agreed—subject, of course, to the approval of the membership. The seamen, however, stalled. Their employers, the shipping-line owners, were reported to be ready to arbitrate, but only if certain conditions were met—primarily, their right to continue to employ those strikebreakers whom they had hired who "followed the sea" as their regular occupation. The seamen demanded that all strikebreakers—"scabs"—be fired. I remember the tired old union president, Andrew Furuseth, looking like an exhausted Norse deity, murmuring: "Never. Never. If I must go to yale, I vill just go to yale. But—no scabs, ever."

The longshoremen went right ahead, submitting to their membership the one question: shall the union agree to submit all issues to binding arbitration? People from various government agencies ran the voting, on only a few hours' notice. A member of the NRA's Regional Labor Board took charge in Seattle. Three Labor Department conciliators were assigned to Tacoma, Portland, and San Pedro. Pat Donoghue, the National Labor Relations Board's very able "chief examiner," handled San Francisco, and I ran the balloting in Oakland and Stockton.

Oakland was easy. The union officers there were experienced and the rank and file understood what they were doing. Ballot boxes were already in place when I arrived, and orderly lines were forming. There were no problems for me to solve. Stockton, however, was very different. This was an upriver port, only recently opened to shipping. The union men there had been longshoremen only briefly; most of them were young, unsuccessful farmers. I had to get the ballot boxes set up, make the ballots themselves available, and persuade the men to vote. Some of them had been drinking, all were noisy, and none, it seemed, had any intention of voting. Finally, to my own astonishment as well as theirs, this Ivy League dude climbed onto a table and roared at them, using profanity that I didn't even realize I knew, and *commanded* them to shut their traps, line up, and vote. To my great relief, they obeyed.

Overall, the longshoremen were in favor of going to arbitration by a four-to-one margin, but this did not end the strike. The seamen had struck in sympathy with the longshoremen (although, to be sure, they had major grievances of their own), and the longshoremen's leaders did not want to let these allies down. But they did want to get back to work. Impatiently they waited while the seamen, the employers' lawyer, and the board argued about three questions.

One I have mentioned, the continued employment of strikebreakers. Another was the employers' use of hiring halls— "fink halls," the seamen called them—wherein seamen seeking work assembled and the shipping company then selected the men it wanted, the men who, said the union's leaders, were least likely to cause any "labor trouble." The third pertained to the union's demand that it be recognized as the bargaining agent of all the seamen. Recognition would have to follow a vote by the seamen indicating their wish to be so represented.

The aforementioned Public Resolution 44 stated that such

votes were to determine which representatives, if any, were desired by "employees of an employer." The shipowners agreed to have a vote taken, but refused to be considered as a single employer. In the voting, therefore, it was necessary to identify each voter as the employee of a particular company. It was also necessary to separate the employees into different logical units: licensed deck personnel, cooks, firemen, and so on. I reported to the Secretary in early August:

> As a result, there was a large envelope which each voter had to fill out, giving the man's name, job, dates of his last voyage, and the company he worked for. . . . The ballot with the single question (Do you wish to be represented by the International Seamen's Union?) was marked by each voter and put into a smaller envelope which was sealed. The small sealed envelope was then placed in the large envelope with the writing on it.
>
> When all the votes are in, the large envelopes will be studied. Votes cast by persons who have been out of work for so long that they could not be considered employees will be thrown away. The other votes will be segregated within each company, by occupation. The large envelope will then be opened and laid aside or thrown away. The small envelopes will be shuffled before they are opened. Secrecy will thus be insured. As a matter of fact, the seamen seemed to have so much faith in the Board's honesty that they flocked to the polls and willingly gave their names and occupations.

It was a long, slow process that took weeks to complete. For the first two or three days, Pat Donoghue and I handled it in San Francisco. I still remember my delight in one man who came to the table I was manning. He was a scowling, swarthy character with a piratical mustache; only a cutlass between his teeth was missing. I took one of those large envelopes, and beside "occupation" I wrote "Cook." (I was right: he just had to be a cook.) Then I asked him his name. "Adams." "Full name, please." Long pause; then: "J. Q. Adams." I yielded to temptation and said again, "*Full* name, please." He glared at me and barked, "John Quincy Adams!" I've always wondered about him!

On Sunday, July 29, came the long-hoped-for break. F. J.

O'Connor, owner of a fleet of "steam schooners" that carried lumber up and down the coast, suddenly announced that he recognized the Seamen's Union as the representative of his two-thousand "unlicensed personnel," that he would rehire all strikers and employ no strikebreakers, and that he would not use any hiring halls. Yet *still* the seamen, whom I described as "undoubtedly abler on the ocean than they are on land," claimed that there were ambiguities in O'Connor's statement that would have to be cleared up to their satisfaction.

That evening I had dinner with the Cushings at their home. During the meal the doorbell rang, and the maid ushered in two large, formidable officers of the Longshoremen's Union. Their patience with the seamen was exhausted. Mr. Cushing took them upstairs to his wife's bedroom, where there was a private telephone. Soon the visitors departed. Mr. Cushing reentered the dining room, pink-faced, eyes shining under his white eyebrows. He said quietly to his wife: "My dear, I think that with your permission I will go on a three-days' drunk." The longshoremen's strike was over: "I'll bet," he said, "that this is the only strike in history to be settled in a lady's bedroom!"

It did not occur to me, or to him, that there was anything odd about the union men coming to him rather than to the chairman of the board, Archbishop Hanna, who had a fine reputation but had clearly outlived it. A longshoreman in Oakland, when I ran the voting there, told me that the board was probably all right because McGrady and Cushing were on it, but "Archbishop Hanna made a speech on the radio the other night all about Jesus! What the hell?" And early one evening, when the aged prelate and I were the last to leave the board's office, he turned to face the empty room and say, very sweetly, "Goodnight, my children."

I left San Francisco on the evening of July 30, with vivid memories of several of the people I had met there. Old Andy Furuseth, sitting on the ground in a park in the morning, waving and shaking his long white locks as the seamen celebrated.

Calm, friendly Pat Donoghue, who would continue to run the seamen's voting. I had met, and liked, the most publicized and in some quarters the most feared person on the whole strike scene, Australian-born Harry Bridges. About him I wrote: "The longshoremen . . . completely trusted Bridges until the 'general strike' and then lost faith in him because it was apparent that the 'general strike' was bad tactics. They continued to have faith in his integrity. Bridges appeared to me to be an intelligent if rather fanatical little man, with a flair for leadership. He went everywhere with a bodyguard of four men, and was alleged to have rejected numerous offers from the employers."

But, as I wrote to my mother, "Probably the *best* experience I had was in coming to know Mr. Cushing. He is a very soft-spoken, dignified seventy-year-old lawyer. He was . . . chairman of the Democratic State Committee when California's vote elected Wilson over Hughes in '16. He is a man whose integrity seems to radiate around him, and who also gives a feeling of great wisdom. His was the strongest San Francisco voice advising Miss Perkins (and through her the President) to keep hands off, and he was eternally right. He refused to compromise for the sake of peace, and stood out for a *just* settlement; and I think he's got it."

The maritime strike was, I think, the last in which I was personally involved. On my return to the capital in early August 1934, I became counsel to the president's Committee on Economic Security, and the drafting and shepherding of legislation became my chief concern. I had already been engaged in the drafting of the Wagner-Lewis unemployment insurance bill of 1934, the provisions of which eventually became Title Nine of the Social Security Act.

Aside from that act, the significant labor bills and laws from 1933 to 1937 were: (1) The National Industrial Recovery Act; (2) The Walsh and Wagner Labor Disputes bills of 1934; (3) The National Labor Relations Act ("Wagner Act"); (4) The

Walsh-Healey Act; (5) The Guffey Bituminous Coal Act; and (6) The Fair Labor Standards bill, introduced in 1937 and enacted in 1938. With the drafting of the first and last of these I had nothing to do. The N.I.R.A. was passed before I went to Washington, and the Fair Labor Standards Act, commonly called the Wage and Hour Law, after I left Washington.

My colleague Gerard Reilly, in 1935, was, I think, the chief draftsman of the Walsh-Healey Act, the law that required that "prevailing wages" be paid to workers on government contract jobs. My diary shows that I "worked with" Gerry a couple of times, but I think I was just reviewing parts of his draft.

We did struggle together with the Guffey bill. This was, basically, John L. Lewis's answer to the Supreme Court's invalidation of the NRA. It purported to establish legislatively what was virtually a whole Code of Fair Competition for the bituminous coal industry. Who wrote the original bill I don't know. It was referred to the Labor Committee of the Senate, of which David I. Walsh was chairman. The bill was vaguely drafted and almost certainly unconstitutional, but for political reasons Roosevelt backed it, even saying publicly that doubts about its constitutionality should not impede its passage. I assume that Senator Walsh asked Miss Perkins to have Reilly and me try to improve the bill; he was acquainted with both of us. We did spend a couple of intense days, simultaneously learning about the economics of the coal industry and tinkering with the proposed legislation. If we improved it, we didn't save it; it was enacted by Congress and promptly held unconstitutional by the Supreme Court.

Senators Wagner and Walsh were the key figures in the prolonged effort, in 1934 and 1935, to produce a labor relations law that would establish a mechanism for protecting labor's right to bargain collectively—a stronger mechanism than the NRA's Labor Board. Wagner was the principal proponent, nationally, of such legislation. Walsh, however, was the senator with whom Wyzanski and I could and did work, for three reasons: his committee chairmanship, his acquaintance with us, and the vehement, almost chemical, ill-feeling between Charlie and Wagner's abrasive secretary, Leon Keyserling. (I disliked Keyserling too, but not with Wyzanski's lifelong bitter scorn; at eighty, Charlie was still seizing an opportunity to write a scathing letter to Keyserling!)

The first "Wagner bill," in 1934, was principally a Keyserling product. It was referred to Walsh's committee, and Wyzanski provided Walsh with a different version, which became the "Walsh bill." It reflected Charlie's comparatively conservative, balanced views, and did not satisfy the union leaders, who pressed for the enactment of the Wagner bill. The latter seemed sure of enactment when, in June 1934, Roosevelt suddenly sent it down the drain by demanding that Congress approve, instead, the aforementioned Public Resolution 44. In the course of the next year, the original Wagner bill was largely rewritten. It was swiftly enacted after the NRA case had invalidated labor's "Magna Carta," section 7a.

Wyzanski had little or no input in the final act, and I none— except for one important phrase. One night back in 1934, when Charlie was drafting the Walsh bill, I came back to the office after supper and, alone, took down from the shelf a heavy old volume of the United States statutes. I looked up the Federal Trade Commission Act of 1914. There I saw what that law forbade: unfair trade practices. I wrote a paragraph for the Walsh bill, outlawing "unfair labor practices," and left my sheet of paper on Wyzanski's desk. In his old age Charlie claimed that he had contributed that phrase to the law, a phrase that was carried over from the Walsh bill to the Wagner bill and eventually to the National Labor Relations Act itself. I did not dispute his claim—but my own memory of that quiet evening on G Street, with that dusty tome on my desk and my own elated feeling of "Eureka!" is and always has been a very vivid one.

Senator Wagner's National Labor Relations Act became law on July 5, 1935, when the president signed it. He also issued the following statement:

This Act defines, as a part of our substantive law, the right of self-organization of employees in industry for the purpose of collective bargaining, and provides methods by which the Government can safeguard that legal right. It establishes a National Labor Relations Board to hear and determine cases in which it is charged that this legal right is abridged or denied, and to hold fair elections to ascertain who are the chosen representatives of employees.

A better relationship between labor and management is the high purpose of this Act. By assuring the employees the right of collective bargaining it fosters the development of the employment contract on a sound and equitable basis. By providing an orderly procedure for determining who is entitled to represent the employees, it aims to remove one of the chief causes of wasteful economic strife. By preventing practices which tend to destroy the independence of labor, it seeks, for every worker within its scope, that freedom of choice and action which is justly his.

The National Labor Relations Board will be an independent quasi-judicial body. It should be clearly understood that it will not act as mediator or conciliator in labor disputes. The function of mediation remains, under this Act, the duty of the Secretary of Labor and of the Conciliation Service of the Department of Labor. It is important that the judicial function and the conciliation function should not be confused. Compromise, the essence of mediation, has no place in the interpretation and enforcement of the law.

This Act, defining rights, the enforcement of which is recognized by the Congress to be necessary as an act of both common justice and economic advance, must not be misinterpreted. It may eventually eliminate one major cause of labor disputes, but it will not stop all labor disputes. It does not cover all industry and labor, but is applicable only when violation of the legal right of independent self-organization would burden or obstruct interstate commerce. Accepted by management, labor, and the public with a sense of sober responsibility and of willing cooperation, however, it should serve as an important step toward the achievement of just and peaceful labor relations in industry.

I've quoted this presidential statement in full because I wrote it. I'm not proud of the sometimes clumsy prose, but I do think that the tone of the message reflects accurately Roosevelt's own feeling about not just this act but the whole subject of labor relations. I certainly don't have him going overboard with enthusiasm. Furthermore, the third paragraph of the statement shows that I had, in one respect at least, become a typical bureaucrat: I was "defending the turf" of my department.

But it was not going to be "my department" much longer. For a year and a half much of my time and thought had been spent on the formulating and nurturing of proposed legislation that in August 1935 became the Social Security Act. A Social Security Board was established to administer that act, and in the fall of 1935 I left the Department of Labor to become the new board's general counsel. My social security story forms the next three chapters.

General Hugh Johnson, director of the National Recovery Administration. Photograph courtesy of the Library of Congress.

Frances Perkins, Secretary of Labor. Photograph courtesy of the
Library of Congress.

Senator Robert F. Wagner of New York. Photograph courtesy of the Library of Congress.

John G. Winant, governor of New Hampshire and later chairman of the Social Security Board. Photograph courtesy of the Library of Congress.

Franklin D. Roosevelt signing the Social Security Act, August 14, 1935, with Representative Robert Doughton (N.C.) of Ways and Means, Ed Witte of the Committee on Economic Security, Senator Robert Wagner (N.Y.), Senator Alben William Barkley (Va.; later vice president under Truman), John Dingell, Senator William H. King (Utah), Secretary of Labor Frances Perkins, Representative David J. Lewis (Md.), and (behind Lewis) Senator Pat Harrison (Miss.) of the Senate Finance Committee. Photograph courtesy of UPI/Bettmann.

Frances Perkins greets F.D.R. upon his return to Washington. Photograph courtesy of the Franklin D. Roosevelt Library.

Chapter 4
The Wagner-Lewis Bill

I HAD NOT been in Washington for a month before I was writing home that "I have been trying to improve the shining hour by studying such things as unemployment insurance, which the Secretary may want to do something about." I did not know, then, that presidential support for unemployment insurance was one of the conditions she exacted from Roosevelt before she would accept the Secretaryship of Labor. Presumably, the president agreed readily enough. After all, at her instigation when she was New York's Industrial Commissioner and he its governor, he had called a conference of governors to discuss the subject. Furthermore, the 1932 Democratic platform had, surprisingly, called for "unemployment and old-age insurance, under State laws."

Surprisingly, there was very, very little knowledge of, or interest in, social insurance at that time. It was a far-out, foreign notion. Oh, yes, I. M. Rubinow, Abraham Epstein, and Paul H. Douglas had written books about it, but who read those books? Many years earlier, to be sure, a plague of industrial accidents had led the states to enact worker's compensation laws, but nobody spoke of these as "social insurance" statutes. I remember a scene in a play I attended in the early thirties; some characters entered the stage carrying placards reading, "We Want Unemployment Insurance," and this got a big laugh from the audience. People who knew that Great Britain had an unemployment insurance system contemptuously referred to it as "the dole."

Nevertheless, bucking the tide or lack thereof, in two states, Ohio and Wisconsin, unemployment insurance bills made legislative progress. The Ohio bill provided that employers must regularly pay contributions, equal to a small percentage of their payrolls, into a statewide unemployment compensation fund. Out of this so-called pooled fund benefits would be paid for a few months to a worker who lost his job and couldn't find another suitable job. The Ohio bill failed of enactment.

Wisconsin was another story. Wisconsin had long been known as one of the truly progressive states,* and then, in the early thirties, it had a Progressive governor, Philip F. La-Follette. In 1932 the legislature enacted a bill different from the Ohio one. Instead of establishing a statewide pooled fund to which all employers would contribute, it required each employer to have an "unemployment reserve" of his own. To it he would contribute and from it he would pay benefits to the workers he laid off. If there were no layoffs, or very few, the reserve would of course mount up. When it reached a certain point, the employer would stop contributing to it. If, later, he laid his employees off and they received unemployment compensation, the reserve would be depleted and he would start contributing to it again.

Thus the Wisconsin law's purpose was not merely to provide a short-term safety net for workers who lost their jobs; it was also to improve economic conditions by inducing employers to stabilize employment. The company that regularly reduced its work force in the summer and rehired in the fall would now find it financially advantageous to schedule production so that there would be no seasonal layoffs. No layoffs, no unemployment compensation benefits to drain the reserve; no diminution of the reserve, no need to make further contributions to it.

---

*Sometime in the thirties, ex-president Hoover was a guest at a luncheon at Harvard. A lady assigned to entertain him, desperately seeking a topic of conversation, mentioned that the dinner plates being used were "Harvard plates," with pictures of Harvard buildings on them. Harvard had started something, she said; now, several colleges had their own. "Wouldn't it be fun," she asked brightly, "to use different college plates for different courses? Soup on the Smith plates; meat or fish on the Yale plates; salad on the Vassar plates; dessert on the Stanford plates!" "And," said the hitherto silent Hoover, "nuts on the Wisconsin plates."

The Wisconsin law did, however, impose a new cost—the payment of contributions—on employers in the state at a time when many were desperate. The Great Depression had the whole country in its grip. Not only might this new cost simply sink some companies into bankruptcy, but many others—those that were in competition with companies in neighboring states—would be sorely hurt. In the winter of 1933, the Wisconsin legislature postponed the effective date of the unemployment compensation law, from July 1, 1933, to July 1, 1934.

The director of the Wisconsin Industrial Commission, Arthur J. Altmeyer, had already selected a young economics instructor, Paul A. Raushenbush, to administer the law, but there was nothing for him to administer. Frustrated, Raushenbush sought advice from his father-in-law. It was all very well, he said, to talk about "unemployment insurance under state laws," but how could a few states act without putting business in those states at a disastrous competitive disadvantage? Some way must be found to induce *all* the states to enact these laws—but what way? How? His father-in-law had the answer.

In the summer of 1933 Raushenbush and his wife visited her parents—Justice and Mrs. Louis D. Brandeis. The justice told them to read and ponder the Supreme Court's decision in the case of *Florida v. Mellon,* decided in 1926. Because of the crucial impact of that case on the development of unemployment insurance in the United States, I must very informally summarize what it concerned and how it was decided.

I think its inception was the Florida "land boom" of the early 1920s. One way to induce rich, elderly northerners to buy new homes in Florida was to remind them that Florida imposed no inheritance taxes. They could come to Florida, bask in the sun, and die in the happy knowledge that their heirs would inherit all their property and the state would get none of it. This was fine as far as Florida was concerned; but those cold Yankee states from which the sybaritic millionaires were emigrating *did* have inheritance taxes, and depended on them to bring in needed revenue. Many state officials, bankers, and real estate people complained that Florida was booming because it had an unfair competitive advantage. They demanded that Congress do something about this.

Congress responded by enacting a federal estate tax statute. This law imposed a federal tax on decedents' estates, but allowed the taxpayer to offset, against the federal tax, most of whatever was owed in state inheritance taxes. So, in effect, the Florida resident was no better off than the New Yorker: his heirs wouldn't have to pay a state inheritance tax but would have to pay the full federal tax. Florida didn't like this one bit. The state brought suit, claiming that this offset provision was unconstitutionally coercing the states to enact inheritance taxes. The United States Supreme Court unanimously rejected Florida's claim and upheld the federal statute.

If Congress could, by a tax-offset device, induce states to enact inheritance tax laws, why couldn't it use the same method to foster the enactment of unemployment insurance laws? This was what Justice Brandeis wanted the Raushenbushes to think about. He was as eager as they were to see unemployment compensation systems established—provided, that is, that they were modeled on the Wisconsin system. The latter, unlike the Ohio "pooled fund" plan, was designed to regularize employment, and this was a purpose long dear to Brandeis's heart. In a speech back in 1911 he had declared that "the paramount evil in the workingman's life is irregularity of employment," adding that "we must have social insurance and . . . create a financial incentive, through the insurance device, to correct the evil of unemployment." So, naturally, he was enthusiastic about the Wisconsin law. As a judge, however, he really could not publicly promote specific legislation.

He did so privately, though. In the early fall he wrote the Raushenbushes explaining the relevance of *Florida v. Mellon* and proposing a federal payroll tax, to be offset by contributions to unemployment reserves. He also spoke to his old friend Lincoln Filene of Boston, telling him that the Raushenbushes might well have the answer to the problem of how to make "unemployment insurance under state laws" possible.

On New Year's Day, 1934, Mr. Filene was visiting his daughter, Mrs. Jouett Shouse, in Washington, and "E.B.," as Mrs. Raushenbush was called, was visiting her parents, the Brandeises. Mr. Filene persuaded the Shouses to let him invite several people to dinner, including Secretary Perkins, Senator Wagner, and E.B., who explained how the tax-offset device would solve the problem. The others agreed, and said that a bill should be drafted accordingly; Wagner promised to introduce it in the Senate, and approved of Miss Perkins's suggestion that David J. Lewis of Maryland should introduce it in the House. Next morning the Secretary, full of enthusiasm, told Wyzanski what had transpired at the dinner.*

And this is where I re-enter the picture. I had innocently spent the latter part of New Year's Day listening to the radio account of Columbia's seven-to-nothing victory over Stanford in the Rose Bowl. And much of January 2, according to my diary, was spent on Capitol Hill and at a Nationality Committee meeting. Sometime during the day, though, Charlie must have told me to get busy drafting a tax-offset bill, for the last diary entry for that day is "unemployment insurance all evening." Meanwhile, E.B. had got hold of Tom Corcoran, who assigned two members of his stable of young lawyers, one of whom was later the greatly distinguished Harvard scholar Paul Freund, to work on the same project.

Neither Paul Freund nor I have any recollection of working together on this project, but we did, delivering a very rudimentary, tentative draft to E.B. on January 4. On the previous day our efforts had been interrupted, and our minds stimulated or confused, by a meeting at the Brandeises' apartment attended by Corcoran, Wyzanski, Isadore Lubin, the Commissioner of Labor Statistics, and E.B. Perhaps fortunately, Miss Perkins did not attend; at a similar meeting two days earlier, Wyzanski told

---

*A biographer of Roosevelt has pointed out how ironic it was that a lasting achievement of the New Deal had its inception in the home of Roosevelt-hating Jouett Shouse: Kenneth S. Davis, *FDR: The New Deal Years, 1933–1937* (New York: Random House, 1986).

me, she had had a "sharp tiff with Miss Brandeis" because she had "expressed doubts about the efficacy of the Wisconsin plan of plant reserves." Battling for her father's beliefs, E.B. continued to insist that the proposed federal payroll tax should be offset only by contributions to plant reserves, not pooled funds. She weakened, a little, when both Altmeyer and her husband, over the telephone, said they thought that states should be allowed to choose one system or the other.

Somebody gave Commissioner Lubin a copy of the Eliot-Freund draft, and he promptly gave it to Abraham Epstein, self-proclaimed and generally acknowledged as *the* expert on social insurance. Mr. Epstein then wrote his own draft, almost identical with what he'd been given except that only pooled fund contributions could be used to offset the federal tax. Lubin called me in, showed the Epstein draft to me, and then set me to work drafting a bill to help him to "increase Labor Statistical work," as I described or misdescribed it in a letter home.

There was no danger of my time and thought being monopolized by unemployment insurance. In that same letter of January 14, 1934, I noted that "I've been to a couple of hearings to testify on rather small naturalization measures before the House Committee; [and] have written my views on what the gov't's policy should be towards labor disputes. . . . A good deal of time has been wasted on the nationality code. . . . Charlie kindly continues to ask my advice on many matters, though I seldom have anything to offer." However, I had begun the letter as follows: "Quite late Sunday night, and here I am at the office, where I stayed till one last night and eleven the night before, feeling very virtuous! It's been the job—labor of love, largely—of redrafting our unemployment bill that's kept me busy nights." I suppose I called it a labor of love because, Freund having faded out of the picture, I could have let our first draft stand; I knew that back in Wisconsin, Paul Raushenbush was preparing his own draft and was about to bring it to Washington.

On the 16th Paul Raushenbush did arrive, and at my office on G Street we went to work. Paul knew much more about unemployment insurance than I did; and as our bill would have to set detailed standards for states to meet in their unemployment insurance laws, we worked from his draft. And now my time *was* monopolized. For six days in succession, according to a diary-like memorandum I later dictated, "Messrs. Raushenbush and Eliot, occasionally assisted by Freund, and with occasional advice from Messrs. Wyzanski and Lubin, worked on the preparation of a final draft. Particularly difficult were the formulation of the sections allowing credits against the tax, and the definition of 'employer' relating to subcontractors. . . ."

The difficulty with the "credits against the tax" was that, to preserve that incentive for regularizing employment which was at the heart of the Wisconsin system, we had to allow the employer to offset, against the federal payroll tax, not only what he was contributing to his unemployment reserve fund but also what he was excused from contributing to it because of his good employment record. (The very length of the foregoing sentence may suggest the problem we faced as we tried to make our draft both exact and understandable.)

Forty-five years later, in the Raushenbushes' published "oral history,"* Paul Raushenbush reminisced about that intense week of joint endeavor.

> The guy I was working with in the Labor Department was Tom Eliot, the assistant solicitor—later a Congressman from Massachusetts and still later a university president. He was an able young attorney who had pretty emphatic ideas of his own. There were a few people who wondered whether such emphatic personalities as we could get together and jointly draft a bill, with lots of controversial issues involved in the drafting. . . . There were a couple of people who sort of stood guard initially to see whether we'd get along. For instance, the solicitor in the Depart-

---

*Paul A. Raushenbush and Elizabeth Brandeis Raushenbush, *Our U.C. Story* (Madison, Wis., 1979).

ment of Labor, Charles Wyzanski, who later became a federal judge ... [and] Paul Freund, now a professor at Harvard. . . . They sort of chaperoned us long enough to see that maybe we would be able to work something out. . . . Tom Eliot and I got along very well. He was a very able guy. A little insistent on his point of view, now and then; but so was I. . . . After we talked it through we managed to iron out most of the substantive problems in drafting, with some compromises in each direction—to get something done. We both knew that there was real urgency about completing our draft.

My own files, aside from the memorandum just referred to, include only a brief mention of that week in a letter of January 21, 1934. "Monday Paul Raushenbush arrived and he and I went to work on a new draft of an unemployment insurance. . . . Tuesday Lincoln Filene—a funny old soul—slung a lunch on our bill, which Paul ran ably. I talked too much. Mr. Dennison [Henry Dennison, tag and paper products manufacturer in Framingham, Mass.] was attractive and intelligent. The discussion was profitable, so we returned to our labors . . . ending each night after midnight."

After we completed the draft that same day, I wrote a brief summary of the bill, for public consumption, omitting unessentials and touching only on the high points. This summary later was the basis of various public statements. Our bill, at that point, imposed a very low payroll tax of 2 percent because Mr. Filene and his enlightened fellow Bay-Staters Dennison and Henry Kendall of the Kendall Company had urged it on us. Now, however, Tom Corcoran called me to say that they had changed their minds: they had, finally, fully understood that the bill would eliminate any competitive disadvantage for firms in states that acted, and so they agreed that the tax rate could be higher. We changed it to 5 percent. They agreed. The next morning I took a copy of the bill to Assistant Secretary McGrady; he sent it quickly to William Green, president of the American Federation of Labor, and assigned his assistant, Dan Tracy, to help obtain A.F. of L. support.

The next day was a busy one. Raushenbush and Tracy and I

called on William Green, who told us that he, personally, was strongly for the bill and would try to get his executive council to support it. In the afternoon the three of us went up to Senator Wagner's office, where we were joined by the businessmen who had attended Mr. Filene's luncheon plus one more, optical goods manufacturer Morris Leeds of Philadelphia. Also present were the A.F. of L.'s representative, William Hushing, and Congressman David J. Lewis.

This was my first encounter with a wonderful man. Davey Lewis had gone to work in the mines of western Maryland, as a breaker-boy, when he was seven. Fifteen years later, with hardly any formal schooling, he had somehow read enough law to escape from the mines and be admitted to the bar. He read much more than law; he may have been self-educated but nobody could deny that he was very well educated. With whitening hair and a face that wrinkled up when he spoke, he was fearless, frank, and funny.

At the conference in Wagner's office, it was Lewis who made the one substantive contribution. After expressing his preference for a truly "Bismarckian" approach in which all forms of social insurance would be merged into one measure, he turned to our draft bill and pointed out a flaw in it: it would require a state to pay unemployment benefits to strikers, whether the state wanted to or not. Paul and I had certainly not intended to make benefits for strikers compulsory, and quickly made the requisite change in the bill. Senator Wagner ended the meeting by expressing his approval of the bill.

That night, according to the memorandum, "Raushenbush, Eliot, and Wyzanski conferred with Secretary of Labor Perkins, who had gone over the bill and favored it very strongly. She said that she would speak to the President about it. She also agreed to call up Abraham Epstein and persuade him to give it his support. . . . Raushenbush then left for Madison."

The bill itself was incomplete, because neither Paul Raushenbush nor I had experience in writing the administrative provisions that any tax statute must contain. A copy was given to

Keyserling, Senator Wagner's secretary, with the understanding—at least it was *our* understanding—that he would ask the
legislative counsel (the professional draftsman) of the Senate
to write those provisions.

On January 30, Wyzanski and I met with Keyserling to discuss labor legislation. When I asked him when the additional
paragraphs in the unemployment compensation tax bill would
be ready, he said there was no hurry; the bill shouldn't be introduced for five or six weeks, and meanwhile he'd write to
"about sixty" people and get their ideas about how to improve
it. This, a day after the Department of Labor had issued a
press release expressing its sponsorship of the bill and Miss
Perkins had spoken on the radio for it!

I was furious. I got a lawyer with Internal Revenue, Harry
Byrne, to write those administrative provisions, and Senator
Wagner overruled his secretary and prepared to introduce the
bill—but I was still seething.

On February 5 I wrote home that for several days, I had

> been feeling exceedingly irritable and prone to make mountains
> out of molehills. Most of this is due to a really very annoying guy,
> one Keyserling, Senator Wagner's dopey secretary, who was as
> nastily obstructive as possible on our bill. ("Our" meaning about
> 3/4 Paul Raushenbush's, 3/16 mine and 1/16 Paul Freund's.) . . .
> Keyserling kept the Department's mimeographers working over-
> time on *his* release to the press, but was furious when I suggested
> he let me know what changes were made in the bill just prior to
> introduction. This in spite of the fact that the Secretary has pub-
> licly endorsed the bill as *we* had written it, and has possibly won
> F.D.'s support. Well, little old Congressman Lewis introduced it
> today, just as it ought to be, and now if its enemies change it that's
> their responsibility. I hope Paul Raushenbush will return to tes-
> tify for it and to help forestall the sabotage that can be expected
> from the bill's "friends"—Keyserling—when it gets to the Sen-
> ate. . . . I'm still sore.

Keyserling was certainly not "dopey." Paul Raushenbush
would surely have described him, too, as "a very able guy." But
he was hard to get along with. Furthermore, he did perhaps

exemplify one side of the clash of principles described by Schlesinger; he had no patience with the Brandeisian decentralizers. I guess that, after all, I was aware that a covert contest was going on to capture the mind of Franklin Roosevelt, for in mid-February I wrote: "One morning I lobbied busily at the House office building for the unemployment insurance bill. F.D.R. hasn't come out for that just as he said he would. Wagner was upset, but Miss P. is sure he just forgot. I'm a little afraid of sabotage however, via Tugwell who is close to Keyserling." And Tugwell, as I have mentioned, was the vocal advocate of the ideas that Schlesinger described as motivating the "first New Deal." In the winter of 1934 he still had the president's ear.

Actually, Keyserling's obstructive tactics did not prevent his boss, Wagner, from introducing the bill in the Senate, but this was just a gesture: revenue bills, the Constitution says, must originate in the House, and this was a revenue bill, levying a 5 percent payroll tax on employers of eight or more people. Of course, we didn't want that tax collected; we wanted it to be offset by unemployment insurance contributions required by state laws. Miss Perkins was eager to have the bill enacted in 1934 so that in 1935 the states could take advantage of its offset provision; most state legislatures had regular sessions only every other year, and were scheduled to hold them in 1935. But I think she was aware, and certainly I was, of major obstacles that would be hard indeed to overcome.

The first of these was the influence of conservative Democrats in Congress. Seniority had brought Southerners to the chairmanship of most committees. Our bill would go first to the House Ways and Means Committee, headed by an elderly, gruff, stubborn North Carolinian, Robert L. Doughton—known as "Muley," though never called that to his face. If the bill reached the Senate it would be referred to the Senate Finance Committee, and that committee was chaired by another Southerner, Pat Harrison of Mississippi. Harrison was not a reactionary; he was more genial than Doughton, but, alas, he was not a friend and admirer of Secretary Perkins. He had once come to the department to see her, without calling ahead. "Miss J" (Frances Jurcovicz), Miss Perkins's Cerberus of a secretary, made no effort to get him in to see the Secretary, did not tell the latter that he was there, and simply left him waiting in the outer office until he got up and left. For this affront he blamed Miss Perkins.

The second obstacle was the position of the president. A firm, definite statement by him to the committee chairmen and the party leaders in Congress that the bill *must* be passed, and it would be passed. The efficacy of a presidential "must list," which had produced an astonishing amount of legislation in 1933, was waning but still had a year or so of life left. But Roosevelt backed and filled. I think he wanted to keep his pledge to Miss Perkins and support the Wagner-Lewis bill. But he knew that to get it through would require the investment of a considerable amount of political capital. And there is some evidence that Rex Tugwell, probably prodded by Keyserling, was putting his oar in to block the bill.

At one point, I would guess after Roosevelt had told him that he'd like to support the bill, Tugwell came up with an idea that would please the president and enable him, Tugwell, to withdraw his objections. This was a notion that if all the state unemployment reserves were invested in United States government securities, the federal government wouldn't have to borrow elsewhere and the currency would be "stabilized" (Tugwell's phrase, and Roosevelt's). In late March I was writing that, urged by "Tugwell, Gardner Means, and the new Assistant Secretary of the Treasury, Marriner Eccles, a radical gent from Utah, the President wants to add a section to the Wagner-Lewis bill to make it work in some way as a stabilizer of the currency: somewhat aside from the chief aim of the bill, but Tugwell says that F.D. will push it through if this section is added, and Miss Perkins is favorably inclined. . . ."

Dr. Lubin, Commissioner of Labor Statistics, was *not* "favorably inclined." He was sure that Tugwell had wildly overestimated the amount of possible state investment; it would take years of full employment, without depletion of the reserves, for the latter to amount to much. He and I went to Tugwell's office; Lubin gave him the facts and figures; Tugwell was dismayed and seemed to be on the verge of apologizing when he suddenly remembered another engagement and fled. That was the end of that idea. Its only effect, or rather the effect of its demise, was to diminish the president's wavering interest in the bill.

Roosevelt did send a letter to Chairman Doughton, saying that he looked upon our bill with approval, but this was a far cry from putting it on his "must list." (Six weeks later, my diary notes that I "sent for and obtained a copy of the President's letter of March 23 favoring the bill after Doughton had carefully said that he had mislaid the original.") A month later the president asked David Lewis to come to the White House, in his note assuring the congressman of his support for the bill. Then, on April 26, I "went to see Congressman Lewis who spoke of his visit at the White House, indicating that the President was talking about appointing a committee to study the whole question of social insurance. Reported this to the Secretary. . . ." This I had dictated to my secretary, for my discreet diary; to my parents I wrote: "My, she [Miss Perkins] blew up the other day, when the President told Mr. Lewis that he was more interested in having all social insurance *studied* than in having the Wagner-Lewis bill passed. 'That man! That man!' She ripped over to the White House and next day he told the press conference that he was 'tremendously' for the bill."

I pause to make two comments on the foregoing paragraph. First, this was the only time I ever heard Frances Perkins say a critical word about Franklin D. Roosevelt. She certainly did not idolize him, but she was working for him, and loyalty was her middle name. Second, recalling what Davey Lewis had said when I first met him, I wondered just a little whether it wasn't Lewis himself who encouraged the president's talk about studying social insurance.

Meanwhile, however, it was Lewis's bill, and more and more it became my bill. Doughton named a subcommittee, chaired by Jere Cooper with Lewis as vice chairman, to hold hearings, and I tried to explain the bill to Lewis. The hard thing to explain was the allowing of an offset (or "credit") against the federal tax for contributions that the employer was excused from paying because of his good employment record. When my oral explanation evoked only a gruff "clear as mud," I knew the bill would have to be changed to clarify this point, for Davey Lewis was not dumb. Earlier, on March 21, I had "made first attempt at rewriting the complicated credit section of the Wagner-Lewis bill" and two days later had done the job. Three weeks later, after the subcommittee had completed its hearings, I "worked on thirteen amendments and sent them to Lewis with a letter."

At the same time, organizing support for the bill, to be expressed at the hearings, was my responsibility—as I wrote home, "keeping track of everything, marshalling the favorable witnesses, coaching them, coaching Lewis in relation to possible questions he might ask, figuring out answers to criticisms, and trying to keep calm in the face of blank misrepresentations by the opponents." On March 21, Miss Perkins ("excessively nervous," as I noted in my diary) was the first witness, followed by Wagner and Harry Hopkins. Those three, of course, were invited by the subcommittee. After them came "my" witnesses: on that day Abe Epstein and Paul Douglas, and later, among others, Marion B. Folsom of Eastman Kodak (subsequently a member of Eisenhower's cabinet), Gerard Swope, Morris Leeds, William Green, and spokespersons for Catholic Charities and the League of Women Voters. After two morning sessions I lunched with Douglas and then Folsom; the latter suggested some of those "thirteen amendments."

Several times the subcommittee met in the evening. Not only "my" witnesses were heard, but opponents also: On March 29 I noted, "Evening hearings. . . . F. H. Willard of Worcester opposed the bill though apparently he was really for it all the time

and merely misunderstood it; Professor Edwin S.
posed it; the National Manufacturers Association's
(well-named) testified for two hours and three-quart
the bill, causing Congressman West to lose his ten
pletely, and failing to cite *Florida v. Mellon.* Hearings adjourned
at midnight. Long walk and talk with Congressman Lewis." A
long day, but I was bright-eyed and bushy-tailed the next afternoon, when I "submitted a legal memorandum and answered
questions for almost an hour." One of the questions was: "How
old are you?"

The hearings were over, but the subcommittee (and I, too)
wanted numerous changes in the bill, and I got busy drafting
them—clearing one or two of these alterations with Paul
Raushenbush, by telephone. Then I took them up to Capitol
Hill and "spent the evening with Mr. Lewis, going over the bill
very thoroughly, discussing its prospects, and learning his
opinions of Daniel Webster, Wendell Phillips, and the plays of
Bernard Shaw." Later that week I "talked with Senator Wagner. . . . He agreed to the suggested amendments, and said the
President had told him he would push the bill."

On April 25, 1934, the subcommittee voted unanimously to
refer the bill to the full Ways and Means Committee without
any recommendation, either for or against it. That committee
met in executive session on May 8, and I certainly felt privileged when I was invited to attend. The reaction was generally
favorable and Lewis told me that he expected the committee
to approve the bill by a vote of 15 to 7, but he was overoptim-
istic. He was not giving enough weight to the opposition of
Chairman Doughton—perhaps because Doughton put on
quite a convincing act of being sympathetic to the purposes of
the bill but just finding it too complex to understand.

Mid-May 1934 saw the end of the Wagner-Lewis bill—or,
rather, its temporary demise, for, as we shall see, it was revived
in 1935. Miss Perkins was slow to give up hope. But a private
talk with Doughton got nowhere, and on May 15 I talked with
Miss Perkins, who said that Doughton continued to oppose the

bill by confusing its provisions, that Senator Harrison was not unfavorable but wanted to sidetrack it for the sake of speedy adjournment, and that Lewis and Wagner were not as strong as they might have been.

The next three weeks were on-again, off-again, but eventually "The Secretary said definitely that the subject of unemployment insurance was so foreign to the South that it appeared that the Senate, Southern Democrats having been canvassed, would not pass the bill. The President is to send a message on the subject, a committee is to be appointed to hold hearings and educate the public, and, if possible, it will be a campaign issue."

Well, it was disappointing. Fortunately, as noted in the previous chapter, I had enough other things to occupy my mind, especially those strikes in Camden and Toledo. Still, as I wrote Berresford,

> this last week has been discouraging and disheartening. Arthur Krock in today's N.Y. Times likened F.D.R. at the present moment to the Roosevelt who was seeking the nomination in 1932— vacillating, uncertain, desiring to placate everyone. I was amused because only last night I told Dave Scoll, who spent the weekend here, that this last week's events had reminded me that I had voted *against* Roosevelt in the 1932 primary." [Dave Scoll and I had campaigned together for Al Smith in 1928.] Well, if the Congressional committee idea *does* go through, I hope Lewis and Wagner are on it and make the most of the Labor Department's services. That should keep me occupied at interesting work, though most people think that shelving social legislation now means the end of it for a good many years.

This gloomy prophecy, of course, was dead wrong. And I was mistaken, too, in both my implicit anger at Roosevelt and my assumption that he would call for the establishment of a special congressional committee to educate the public. He did not intend to shelve social insurance legislation. On the contrary, he appointed a committee to formulate and propose it. This was not a committee of senators and representatives, but of Cabinet members—and its chairman was Frances Perkins.

Expecting the president to go the congressional-committee route, she had told me that she hoped I would be counsel for whatever committee was appointed. Now she could realize that hope, and she did so. When I returned from the San Francisco adventure in the summer of 1934 I was still Associate Solicitor of the Department of Labor, but I was also, and primarily, counsel to the President's Committee on Economic Security.

Chapter 5

The Social Security Act

Today the phrase "social security" has come to mean old age insurance, perhaps with Medicare thrown in. But the bill that became law in 1935 included many other things: grants to the states for the needy aged and the needy blind, for child welfare and public health programs, and for aid to families with dependent children, plus a payroll tax with offset provisions to induce the states to establish unemployment insurance systems. I think it was only after World War II that "social security" came to connote old age insurance, not too surprisingly, because by that time most of us had social security cards and numbers to evidence our participation in the old age insurance program.

Still, it was social insurance, not "welfare," that the president specifically mentioned when, in a message to Congress on June 15, 1934, he said: "Among our objectives I place the security of the men, women, and children of the nation first . . . security against the hazards and vicissitudes of life. . . . Next winter we may well undertake the great task of furthering the security of the citizen and his family through social insurance. . . . I am looking for a sound means which I can recommend to provide at once security against several of the great disturbing factors in life—especially those which relate to unemployment and old age." Two weeks later he issued an Executive Order establishing the Committee on Economic Security (naming the Secretary of Labor as chairman—yes, chairman, not chairperson or chair), directing it to report to him in December its recommendation of "proposals which in its judgment will promote greater economic security."

As I noted in the last chapter, when Miss Perkins told me that the Wagner-Lewis bill would be set aside and a new committee appointed, she had added that this might be a campaign issue in the upcoming congressional elections. And I was already enough of a politician to stop being annoyed with Roosevelt's waffling on Wagner-Lewis and instead to marvel at his political skill. Certainly the individual's economic security, and the promise to promote it, made a good campaign issue—and because the committee wasn't to report until after the election, there was nothing specific that the Republicans could attack.

There were other compelling political reasons for promising to take action. In increasing numbers, people—especially the elderly—were flocking to the banner of Dr. Francis Townsend, who was advocating handouts of $200 a month to everybody sixty or older, to be financed by something he called a transactions tax. The zeal of the good doctor's converts was intense, and Townsend Clubs were blossoming all over the place. Meanwhile, in the wings was Senator Huey Long, the self-styled Kingfish, recently the autocratic governor of Louisiana. Unlike most despots, Huey Long was not only smart and vulgar but funny, and hence more appealing and more dangerous. His slogans were "Share the Wealth" and "Every man a King," and it was pretty generally assumed that he had his eye on the presidency in 1936. The economy was improving somewhat, but there was a chance that in 1936 times would still be so hard that either the Democrats would dump Roosevelt or both of the old parties could be defeated by an independent candidate shouting populist slogans.

Times were indeed hard, especially for those whom Roosevelt targeted as objects of social insurance: the unemployed and the aged. Many millions were unemployed.* Millions more

---

*It's often said that the New Deal largely failed to reduce unemployment until World War II sparked a big defense buildup. This assumes, however, that "unemployment" means not having a job in the private sector or in some traditional governmental task like soldiering or school teaching. I've never seen why the millions working in Works Progress Administration jobs were still called "unemployed." They accomplished a lot (new schoolhouses, new post

were old and destitute. In the previous decade most states, often spurred on by the Fraternal Order of Eagles, had enacted old age pension laws, under which monthly grants to the needy aged enabled them to live at home rather than be herded into public poorhouses. Alas, the Depression had depleted every state's resources, and those monthly payments had shrunk and shrunk again, from $30 down to a national average of $16.28, and, in thirteen states, less than ten dollars. Starvation was a reality in the Great Depression.

So the Committee on Economic Security had a big job on its hands. It was composed of Miss Perkins, Relief Administrator Hopkins, Secretaries Morgenthau of the Treasury and Wallace of Agriculture, and Attorney-General Homer Cummings. The last, as far as I can recall, never came to any meetings; to most of them he sent the assistant to the attorney-general, Alexander Holtzoff. Morgenthau was a frequent absentee, his representative in some of the later meetings being the very liberal and effective Assistant Secretary, Josephine Roche.

In a letter I wrote, rather disrespectfully, that "the cabinet committee met at noon for a two-hour session on old age pensions. We have a lunch of sandwiches, coffee, and pie brought in and get on a very informal basis. Harry Hopkins, it seems to me, usually talks like an awful kid [I wonder, now, what he thought of *me*!], very grandiose and exaggerated in his ideas which are often half-baked. . . . Wallace (who couldn't eat the sandwiches because he's in a vegetarian phase) has a lot of charm and Miss Perkins sticks to the point. I can't hand Morgenthau much on slight acquaintance." No mention of the attorney-general.

I was at that meeting, and many others, in my capacity as counsel to the committee. Unfortunately, though, it was not my only job. Having hired Edwin E. Witte of Wisconsin as its executive director, the committee established a Technical Board

---

offices, successful theatrical productions, a series of state guidebooks, for example), and if their hours were a little short and their pay low, they were paid not only in cash but in revived self-respect.

of so-called experts, headed by Arthur Altmeyer, who had come from Wisconsin to be Assistant Secretary of Labor; I was made a member of that board, served on its unemployment insurance subcommittee, and filled in for the absent Lubin on its public employment and relief subcommittee. "The last two nights have seen late meetings," I wrote on September 28, "Midnight last night, and another begins in a few minutes which may last even longer." I really should have asked Miss Perkins to excuse me from these committee assignments, just as, later that fall, I should have declined a number of invitations to speak before various groups. The legal job for the Committee on Economic Security was really enough.

The primary task, of course, was drafting a bill. I couldn't do much about that until the committee decided what it wanted to propose, but I had to be ready with tentative drafts for them to discuss. What I wanted most was the inclusion, in any new bill, of the previous year's Wagner-Lewis bill. What puzzled me most was how to implement the promises of the 1932 Democratic platform, and now of the president, for old age insurance.

The committee's staff, under Ed Witte, from the University of Wisconsin, was gathering detailed information about social insurance in other countries. After all, the idea was far from new. Bismarck had established a comprehensive system in Germany, way back in 1889. "Compulsory contributory old age insurance laws," as the committee styled them, had come into effect in most of Europe in the first thirty years of this century, among them France in 1910, Italy in 1919, and Great Britain in 1925. These laws differed in various respects: in all the continental countries, for example, old age benefits were measured by the amount of the recipient's former wages, while in Britain every covered worker received the same amount.

But in one respect—and this is what impressed me as I sought to learn more about the subject I was grappling with— all the European systems were alike. All were "contributory," but in every one of them the "contributions" from employers and employees were not enough to meet the full cost of the program. The government, out of its general funds, made up the difference. I knew that the president was intent on having a contributory system here: I could only hope that this was the kind he would prefer.

As I waited to be given something definite to draft, I thought mostly about the omnipresent question of constitutionality—not just of old age insurance but of everything that would be in whatever bill the committee would recommend.

The Supreme Court had not yet started to strike down New Deal statutes (from 1935 to 1937 they nullified eight), but the lower courts were busy doing so, and every knowledgeable New Deal lawyer thought he could count the votes of the justices: Brandeis, Cardozo, and Stone to sustain most New Deal laws, the "battalion of death," McReynolds, Butler, Van-Devanter, and Sutherland, to call them unconstitutional, and Roberts and Chief Justice Hughes *probably* siding with the McReynolds foursome. I did feel, however, that there were two schemes that the committee might propose which would gain the Court's approval; judicial precedent was on our side.

One of these two schemes, of course, was the Wagner-Lewis unemployment compensation plan, for which the precedent was *Florida v. Mellon*. The other was having the federal government make grants to the states for specified welfare purposes. In the twenties, Congress had enacted the Maternity Act, under which annual grants were made to states for their maternal-and-child-care programs, if those programs complied with the conditions and met the standards prescribed in the federal statute. This law was challenged as being unconstitutional because it "coerced" the states to act, but the Supreme Court unanimously upheld it—the opinion, surprisingly, being written by the very conservative Justice Sutherland.

As far as I was concerned, then, the committee would be safe in recommending that a new overall "economic security bill" should include both the Wagner-Lewis provisions and grants to the states to increase the amounts they could pay to the needy aged and destitute (or broken) families with dependent children—"mother's aid," it was called then ("welfare," now). But what in the world could be devised to carry out the president's wish for a contributory old age insurance program that would pass judicial muster? I wasted some time thinking about this, and even drafted a half-baked measure that, as I now recall it, would finance the annuities by poll taxes (page Margaret Thatcher!). I don't think I showed that draft to anyone, however.

Meanwhile, two people on the Technical Board's old age insurance subcommittee, the amiable J. Douglas Brown of Princeton and the acerbic Barbara Armstrong of Berkeley, were formulating proposals for a national scheme to be financed by payroll taxes. They insisted that the Democratic platform's pledge was utterly impractical: "under State laws," the platform had said, but so many people move from state to state during a lifetime that actuarial predictions would certainly be impossible and proper record-keeping almost certainly so. And Mrs. Armstrong, in particular, was a fierce advocate of national action on all fronts.

I could not honestly assure the committee that a national plan for old age insurance would be upheld by the Supreme Court. Oh, yes, if I were a judge I'd say it was a valid law, an exercise of the powers that the Constitution gives to Congress, to tax and to spend for the general welfare. But I was aware of what judges were doing to the Agricultural Adjustment Act, which levied a "processing tax" on foodstuff processors and allocated the proceeds to farmers who reduced their acreage or livestock production.

The Supreme Court hadn't yet nullified that statute, but the lower federal courts were showing the way. Already many federal injunctions had been issued (there were sixteen hundred in all) forbidding collection of the tax. I was ready to bet that the Supreme Court would strike this law down, on the ground that, although it pretended to be a tax-and-spend statute, it was in reality a federal scheme to regulate agricultural production, and the Constitution gave Congress no such authority. So, with respect to old age insurance, wouldn't the Court say that a law levying a payroll tax and spending the proceeds in paying old age benefits was really nothing else but a federal insurance scheme to provide annuities to the elderly, and that the Constitution gave Congress no authority to go into the insurance business?

I had to admit, though, that old age insurance under state laws was an impractical notion, so the committee would have to recommend some kind of national plan. It's surprising to remember how little time the committee spent on that whole subject. When the time came for final drafting, I "farmed out" the task of writing the tax provisions, and those relating to the investment of old age reserves, to Alanson Willcox of the Treasury Department. We then worked together to conform the definitions in his draft (of "employee," "employer," "employment," and the like) with those in the benefits section that I was writing. And I asked my Labor Department colleague, Katherine Lenroot, head of the Children's Bureau, to prepare the aid-to-dependent-children and child-care provisions that the committee wanted. She did as she was asked, but the resulting product needed a lot of careful revision. I did not spend enough time doing that. I was just too busy once again with what was, for me, the all-engrossing subject of unemployment insurance.

Not only for me. Barbara Armstrong, straying off her own turf, was vehemently leading a drive for a national unemployment insurance system. The committee's high-ranking Advisory Council, meeting for a week in November and a second week in December, virtually ignored all subjects other than unemployment insurance, as its members argued the comparative merits of a national system, Wagner-Lewis, and a hybrid federal "subsidy plan." Before saying more about that council, I should explain why I felt confident that the committee would reject any proposal for a national system.

On August 12, 1934, before the committee had had its first

meeting, Miss Perkins invited Witte, Altmeyer, and me to accompany her to the White House. We were with the president for nearly an hour, in the course of which one of us mentioned that some people were suggesting that unemployment insurance should be a federal function. "Oh no," said Roosevelt quickly, "we've got to leave all that we can to the states. All the power shouldn't be in the hands of the federal government. Look—just think what would happen if all the power *was* concentrated here, and *Huey Long* became president!"

Miss Perkins's summons had come while I was writing a letter home, and on my return from the White House I continued it, in some excitement:

> Well well! Just back from the White House, where Miss P. took Altmeyer, Witte, and me to see the President! He has a huge hand and a big head; looks young (brown hair on top) and vigorous, and seemed nervous, talking quickly and making queer faces. He was . . . in agreement with having the Wagner-Lewis bill device used in the coming program. He wanted the use of gov't funds limited as much as possible, preferring "contributions." . . . He seemed particularly keen about the investment of the funds, with the issue of currency against the accumulated reserves in time of depression. [That Tugwell idea again!] "Expansion of the currency—mustn't call it inflation," he said with a grin. . . . In the course of the discussion, Miss Perkins mentioned not putting too big a load on industry: they couldn't stand it. "But they're in the black," said the President. Later, *in re* getting a big business man to head the Advisory Council and reassure industry, she began repeating some of the conservative arguments. They can't expand unless they can reasonably expect huge profits. "Not any more," interjected F.D. And again, their profits will be so diminished that they won't be able to pay dividends. "Abnormal dividends," smiled the President.

At that meeting, as far as I can remember, I made only one remark. The conversation had turned to the question of who should be chairman of the Advisory Council, the establishment of which, along with the Committee on Economic Security itself, had been declared in the Executive Order. I recall getting up my nerve and saying, "Owen Young." President Roosevelt turned to gaze at me with an expression I interpreted as "well, look what the cat brought in." I feared—though it did not worry me much—that the president was annoyed, but much later realized that he may just have been surprised that I mentioned Owen Young, who was one of three businessmen Roosevelt had very privately and confidentially consulted before issuing the Executive Order.

For me, though, the big things about that hour at the White House were the mere fact of being there and the president's stated preference for unemployment insurance "under state laws." I thought that this meant that there'd be no trouble in getting the Wagner-Lewis approach to be recommended by the committee. I was mistaken.

The Technical Board's unemployment insurance subcommittee was chaired by Bryce Stewart, of Industrial Relations Counselors, Inc. Like Mrs. Armstrong, he was vehemently in favor of having a national system of unemployment insurance. When the two of them came to understand that this would not have Roosevelt's approval, they proposed, instead, a "subsidy plan." Their proposal was about as close to a national plan as it could be, for in it the "subsidy"—the grant to a state to finance unemployment insurance benefits—was conditioned on having the state law, and its administration, comply with a great number of detailed federal directives and restrictions. Both Stewart and Mrs. Armstrong argued for the subsidy plan at council meetings; I spoke up, more than once, for the Wagner-Lewis approach. In answering questions about the constitutionality of the two proposals, I felt severely handicapped; I could say confidently that Wagner-Lewis would be sustained by the Court, but I would not explain why I was confident. I knew that I must not mention Justice Brandeis.

Owen D. Young did not become chairman of the Advisory Council—"too conservative," Roosevelt had muttered. That appointment went to President Frank Graham of the University of North Carolina. I came to know him in later years, first when he headed the War Labor Board and still later when he was a senator. He was a fine person—a true Southern gentleman and a compassionate, caring, intelligent progressive, and that's quite a combination. But in 1934 my juvenility was showing when I wrote home about him and the Advisory Council: "The employers . . . are all right, but the labor men are awful and President Graham, while he's called a Red by Southerners, thinks at the usual Southern pace. Grace Abbott [former director of the U.S. Children's Bureau] has lots of good ideas but is always asking for explanations and then not listening to them." Curiously, in view of my subsequent association with him, I never mentioned another member of the council, Governor John G. Winant of New Hampshire.

A later letter, on December 11, reported:

> The Advisory Council met in full session the last three days of the week, and we had a long and bitter battle. We killed one big business scheme but lost, 9–7, Friday afternoon on the issue of whether to go through with the Wagner-Lewis bill or adopt a subsidy plan instead. Saturday the subsidy boys tried to press their advantage by getting the council to commit itself on a detailed bill, with the result that there was a lot of new wrangling, much rather angry argument, (Grace Abbott shouts and spares no feelings!) and finally a withdrawal of Friday's action and no specific endorsement or rejection of either plan—a relief!

Actually, at that final meeting the council debated more than Wagner-Lewis *v.* subsidy plan. The members voted against recommending that states require employees to contribute to unemployment compensation funds—another close division on an issue that aroused strong feelings.

In between meetings and heated arguments I was hurriedly drafting bills and statements, as ordered by the Committee on Economic Security—all of them concerning unemployment insurance. Again, it does seem very strange that so very little time was spent by the committee, the Advisory Council, or me on much the largest program in the Social Security Act, namely, old age insurance!

The committee was not ready to report to the president on

December 1, as originally required. He extended its life, by another Executive Order—and then put the pressure on. In his annual message to Congress on January 4, 1935, he spoke of "security against the major hazards of life. . . . A comprehensive survey of what has been attempted or accomplished in many Nations and in many States proves to me that the time has come for action by the national Government. I shall send to you, in a few days, definite recommendations based on these studies." In a few days! The various Technical Board subcommittees hadn't yet reported; the committee itself hadn't reached firm conclusions. It was thirteen days later that the president sent his special message on economic security to Congress. But before he did so an unexpected event occurred that had a lasting effect on the social security program in the United States.

The committee had agreed on recommending a national old age insurance system based primarily on payroll taxes on employers and taxes on employees' wages and salaries. Miss Perkins and Harry Hopkins had spent an evening with the president and left believing that they had his full approval of the comprehensive bill they were discussing, including its old age insurance provisions. In that belief they had a Committee Report drafted, and on January 17 the White House issued a statement summarizing that report.

The statement included this passage: "We suggest that the Federal Government make no contribution from general revenues to the [old age reserve] fund during the years in which income exceeds payments from the fund, but that it guarantee to make contributions, when the level of payment [of benefits] exceeds income from contributions and interest, sufficient to maintain the reserve at the level of the last year in which income exceeded payments." Two days earlier, a press release had been prepared for the committee which mentioned the committee's belief that no "contributions from general revenues" would be required before 1965.

Miss Perkins had obtained the signatures of all the other

members of the committee, but the report had not yet been delivered at the White House, when Henry Morgenthau, Secretary of the Treasury, saw a copy of that press release. He demanded a special meeting of the committee, at which he announced that he was withdrawing his signature: to say that this was an insurance system, he thundered, and then thirty years hence have the federal Treasury subsidize it out of general revenues was a fraud on the taxpayer. Wallace rolled his eyes and looked at the ceiling. Harry Hopkins and Mr. Holtzoff stared, open-mouthed. Miss Perkins, her voice rising, said "But Henry! But *Henry!*" Morgenthau interrupted her by slamming his hand down on the table and shouting, "This is Henry Morgenthau, Jr., speaking and these are his opinions!" Late the same day word came from the White House that the bill that was supposedly ready for introduction would have to be changed; the taxes for old age insurance would have to be increased, so that ultimately the reserve fund would be nearly six times greater than the committee had contemplated and no "government contribution" would be necessary, ever.

I asked Miss Perkins why the president had ordered this, when he'd earlier agreed to the committee's plan as outlined to him by her and Hopkins. She said: "Oh, I can guess. Right after breakfast Henry's sure to appear in the president's bedroom, insisting on this change. The president tells him to go away. He comes back to the White House at noon and tells his story again. And then about four o'clock, when the president's getting tired, he puts his head in the door *again*, and the president says, 'Oh, all right, Henry, all right!' "

That was her interpretation, uttered quite cheerfully, of Roosevelt's seeming *volte-face*. I'm not so sure: I remembered, then, a remark Roosevelt had made at that conference in the Oval Office in August: "No dole—mustn't have a dole." I thought Morgenthau might have had a very quick, supportive response when he told his chief that the committee was proposing a "dole" in 1965. On the other hand, there was the White House itself issuing the summary quoted above, which didn't mention 1965, to be sure, but did call for a "dole" when necessary to balance the reserve fund's income against its outgo.

I have gone into this incident at some length, because it sheds a little light on a question that has bothered me from time to time, especially when the future of Social Security is being argued in Congress and gloomy prophets say that some day the whole system will go bankrupt. When, in the seventies, Congressman James Burke of Massachusetts introduced a bill to provide that the federal government, out of its general funds, should contribute to the social security reserves, I wrote him the following letter, which he inserted in the Congressional Record:

> In 1935, as counsel to the President's Committee on Economic Security, I drafted the bill which, with some revisions, became the original Social Security Act. I now applaud your effort to supplement old age insurance funds with general revenues, and thus to get rid of the notion that the system should be forever "self-supporting."
>
> All the members of the committee and its large staff of experts agreed on the contributory principle: the ultimate beneficiary should contribute a part of the cost of his eventual old age annuity. They agreed, too, that for a while the rest of the cost should be borne by employers, through payroll taxes. But they assumed that before long, others than employers would also contribute—in other words, that both payroll taxes and income taxes would supplement the employee's contributions.
>
> All, that is, agreed, except the Secretary of the Treasury, Henry Morganthau. When he saw a proposed press release saying that [no] general fund contributions would be required before 1965, he objected, and persuaded the President that the rates of payroll and earnings taxes should be raised, to make the system forever "self-supporting." The rest of the Committee and the staff greatly regretted this, for the earnings tax, while necessary to effectuate the contributory principle, is a regressive tax and should be held at a very low rate."

That letter did not tell the whole story. Perhaps I should have admitted that in his special message to Congress the president had said that funds for old age insurance "should not come from the proceeds of general taxation." So, defenders of the present system can argue that Congress intended that it should forever rely solely on "contributions"—payroll taxes. However, this argument can be refuted. In 1939, Congress amended the Social Security Act, reducing the payroll tax to the point where the actuaries predicted that contributions from "the proceeds of general taxation" would be needed by the nineteen-eighties. This amendment was proposed by a committee of experts headed by J. Douglas Brown. It had the full support of the president. (Where was Morganthau?!) Its enactment, it seems to me, counters the notion that the system's permanent dependence solely on payroll taxes is a basic principle "carved in stone" and forever unchangeable. I would like to see the day come when that regressive tax is again reduced.

Now, to get back to January 1935: copies of the sixty-three-page "Economic Security Bill" went up to Capitol Hill and were duly introduced by Senator Wagner and Representative Lewis. However, "Muley" Doughton, as chairman of the House Ways and Means Committee to which the bill would be referred, obtained an extra copy of the bill, "introduced" it by dropping it into the hopper in the well of the House, and persuaded the House clerk to give it a lower number than Lewis's. This petty exercise of power—Ways and Means was recognized as the most powerful House committee—made it look as though the bill had been first introduced by Doughton, and the press was fooled and called it the Wagner-Doughton bill. Mr. Lewis was hurt and angry, but he swallowed hard and went to work to understand every sentence of the bill and to master the arguments in favor of it. It may not have been called the Wagner-Lewis bill, as it should have been, but when eventually it was debated, the House gave Lewis a standing ovation as he stumped down the aisle to speak in its behalf.

Some newspapers were off the beam, too, in their criticism of the bill after it was introduced and its contents were made public. They assailed the new bill as a hodgepodge, an ill-drafted legislative monstrosity. Their criticisms on this score were uninformed. The chief complaint was that various subjects were scattered throughout the measure: thus, one chapter or "title" imposed a tax for old age insurance, while the provisions for old age benefits appeared in a separate title many pages distant. The critics did not know—or perhaps they did—that this awkward arrangement was deliberate. It was designed to make it easier for the Supreme Court to sustain the measure's validity—not to fool the Court, but to give the justices a technical peg on which to hang their hats if they so desired. Meanwhile, some social security experts joined the chorus, citing other examples of bad draftsmanship; again, their examples did not prove their point. They objected to substance, not form; they preferred ways of promoting unemployment compensation different from the tax-offset device included in the bill.

Yet the original bill was certainly not well drafted. It was indeed a hodgepodge—not of unrelated subjects, but of drafts prepared by various people, drafts that I either accepted *in toto* (such as the old age tax provisions hurriedly prepared in the Treasury Department) or edited far too hastily (the welfare titles written in the Children's Bureau, for example). Inevitably, too, it reflected a heedless failure to resolve many small but significant policy issues that had been discussed little or not at all by the president's committee. Drafting is not just a technical job; it requires foreseeing every reasonably possible question that may arise and eliminating every ambiguity.

This I really learned that winter from a great and unsung teacher. He was Middleton Beaman, legislative counsel of the House of Representatives. A tense, caustic, redheaded Yankee, he reminded me of a Vermont schoolmarm; and it was indeed this role that he played when he and I appeared, day after day, at the executive sessions of the Ways and Means Committee.

The committee's procedure was to "read the bill, paragraph by paragraph." No sooner was a sentence read, however, than Mr. Beaman was on his feet asking questions: where the bill said that "employees" should receive old age benefits, did it mean to include American employees stationed abroad? If the committee members said "No," then Mr. Beaman, terrier-like, would ask: "What about a contractor in Detroit who sent his regular crew on to a job for a few days in Windsor, Ontario? What about seamen on the Great Lakes? A cook on a ship that went from Seattle to Alaska, through Canadian waters?" He insisted on answers, and the committee members generally complied.

Mr. Beaman (I never heard anyone call him anything except "Mr. Beaman") and I not only sat together at the executive sessions of the Ways and Means Committee; we worked prodigious hours in his quiet basement office, sometimes joined by his Senate counterpart, Mr. [Charles F.] Boots, and by Alanson Willcox of the Treasury. "Working 12 hours a day," I wrote home in mid-February, "and I have enjoyed it. It consisted first of several days with the House and Senate Legislative Counsel—the boss a Harvard man named Middleton Beaman. I ate crow steadily while they tore a lot of the bill to pieces with gusto and well-merited scorn. It was too interesting, mentally, for me to worry about it for a while, and then when I began to feel that I was really a complete dub and had done a rotten job, Beaman took me aside and said he'd like to have me working with him permanently! So I felt better, though I've learned several lessons about trying to do too much myself and being over-hasty."

This educational process continued for several weeks, for nearly every day the committee asked that some section or paragraph of the bill be changed. Once, on a Friday, several members expressed dismay that, in the bill, the old age benefits stopped at the recipient's death; no provision was made for his widow. (It was assumed that the recipient would be male!) The chairman then directed Mr. Beaman and me to draft new sections to include benefits for widows. Over the weekend Mr. Beaman, Alanson Willcox and I worked late into the night, even getting an actuary to advise us. On Monday, when we presented our draft to the committee, the members discussed it for five minutes and then voted to drop the whole subject. Not until the law was amended in 1939 did old age insurance become the "Old Age and Survivors' Insurance" that we know today.

Before going into executive session, the Ways and Means Committee had held well-publicized hearings, and the Senate Finance Committee also held hearings. The star witness, who testified for two full days before each committee, was Ed Witte. He was a walking encyclopedia of information concerning welfare statutes and social insurance. The task of organizing the favorable non-governmental witnesses was handed to Ed McGrady. I attended some of the hearings in the Senate and the first few days of them in the House.

On January 26, 1935, I wrote: "Hearings all week, a little strain when Miss Perkins was testifying as I had to stick next to her and whisper answers to questions they asked her. She and the blind (literally) Sen. Gore had an amusing time arguing about 'the struggle for existence,' Miss Perkins stoutly maintaining that the only reason the sons of the poor reached positions of trust more often than the sons of the rich is that there are more of 'em!"

This letter continued: "Between times I share an office, off the Senate Finance Committee rooms, with a very nice Mississippian named Calhoun, retained as expert for the Senate Committee, and he and I go to see Pat Harrison now and then. . . . I also confer periodically with Wagner, whose intellect is not of the kindergarten variety, and have to waste hours with the megalomaniacs of the F.E.R.A. [Relief Administration] who want to change the bill and give Hopkins complete power to toss millions around for old age pensions just as he sees fit." This was written before I moved my base of operations to Mr. Beaman's quarters in the bowels of the House Office Building.

My recollections of the Ways and Means Committee's executive sessions, when they considered the bill title by title, section by section, sub-paragraph by sub-paragraph, include a number of things that still make me smile. One is of the modest betting contest I had with Mr. Beaman. On some days the committee would cover several pages of the bill, and on other days only a few lines. Before a session, as the members were assembling, Mr. Beaman would bet me how far the committee would progress that morning. He won regularly, and it took me several days to catch on. Mr. Beaman based his predictions not on the complexity of the bill's subject matter but on the behavior of one committee member as he first entered the room. That one member was Fred Vinson of Kentucky, later Chief Justice of the United States. If Vinson, on entering, walked directly to his seat, said an amiable "good morning," and began perusing the bill, we were pretty sure to have a productive day. If, however, he came in either scowling and growling or whispering jovial stories to a couple of his colleagues, the morning could be counted as lost.

Vinson was the dominant influence, but there were other congressmen who could hold things up or make them march. The able and ever-courteous Jere Cooper of Tennessee, reluctant to say that he opposed anything, would wrinkle his brows most painfully and say: "I'm just—ah wah—just a country boy, and I just can't seem—ah wah—can't seem to *understand*." On the Republican side, old Allen Treadway, the big bull-voiced hotel-keeper from Massachusetts, took a vast interest in two relatively small matters, forcing each to be discussed for a whole morning. One was the plight of hotels that would be subject to a payroll levy, in competition with those "cabins" that preceded today's motels, where there were no bellboys or waitresses and so no payrolls to tax. The other was whether janitors in private schools should have social security. Why this was worth three hours of discussion was a mystery; Mr. Treadway's interest seemed to stem from the fact that his grandson attended an "ivy" boarding school, but surely it was not on the verge of bankruptcy.

On the Ways and Means Committee in 1935 was another Massachusetts man who later attained national distinction as

Speaker of the House—John W. McCormack. He took little part in the discussion, but his quick thinking saved an important section of the bill from temporary extinction. Angered by the committee's refusal to exempt incorporated farms from the unemployment compensation tax, a rural member suddenly moved to eliminate all provisions relating to unemployment compensation. The roll was called, and the vote stood at eight to eight. Up to that moment, there had been no proxy voting or even the mention of such a possibility, but now came Treadway's deep and portentous voice: "I have the proxy of our colleague, Dr. Crowther, and he votes aye." Instantly McCormack, looking blandly at the ceiling, spoke in a rapid monotone: "I have the proxies of Mr. Cullen and Mr. Sullivan and they both vote no." Sauce for the gander!

But this was not the only time that unemployment compensation came under attack. At a meeting attended by a bare majority of the committee, an amendment was approved by a close vote that would have nullified the whole notion, so dear to Brandeis, that unemployment insurance could be used to foster the stabilization of employment. The amendment struck from the bill the clauses that allowed the employer to offset, against the federal tax, the amount of contributions he was excused from paying to the state because of his good employment record. This I reported to Altmeyer—I think properly, even though the committee's sessions were confidential, for I was still in the Labor Department and Altmeyer was Assistant Secretary. I had not foreseen what then happened. Altmeyer telephoned the news to Paul Raushenbush in Wisconsin; Raushenbush telephoned it to a Wisconsin employer, Roger Sherman Hoar, a man with an impressive Massachusetts family background; Hoar telegraphed his friend Congressman Treadway of Massachusetts, demanding that the committee reverse its action.

Treadway came to the next meeting in a towering rage. How could the committee proceed when there were leaks like this? Who could be trusted? Other members took up the cry. All eyes focused not on me, but on the other outsider who attended the closed sessions, Ed Witte—of Wisconsin. He looked totally bewildered. He did not know what had happened. Neither did I. While the angry chorus continued—I think they expected Witte to confess—I slipped out, telephoned Altmeyer, and learned what had taken place. Then I came back, asked to be heard, and without naming anyone said that I was responsible for the information having leaked out.

Instantly the atmosphere changed. At least three congressmen, including Treadway, praised me fulsomely for so courageously confessing. Witte became my grateful friend. Altmeyer got off scot-free. One representative muttered to me, when the session ended: "I know how it is; when those newspaper guys get after you it's very hard not to answer their questions."

The Ways and Means Committee made a number of other substantive changes in the bill. They added a "title" for aid to the needy blind, and at Lewis's insistence inserted a provision for "voluntary insurance" covering people not covered by the old age insurance sections. Another change concerned nomenclature. In the original bill, administration of the social insurance programs was entrusted to a "Social Insurance Board," while the various welfare programs were the responsibility of the Department of Labor. The committee voted to put almost everything together under one board. But, said a congressman, then it wouldn't be a Social *Insurance* Board, because grants-in-aid to help the needy aren't insurance. Another congressman—I wish I could remember who it was—remarked, "Let's call it the Social *Security* Board, then." Everyone agreed, and to make things consistent, they voted to change the last sentence of the bill, which was "This Act may be cited as the Economic Security Act," to "This Act may be cited as the Social Security Act."

Particularly among the Southern representatives there were frequently expressed objections to the detailed federal standards that a state had to meet to qualify for a grant or a tax offset. Some of those standards, especially those requiring that state programs be staffed by civil service personnel, were stricken from the bill. I was glad that I'd so vehemently opposed the subsidy plan. I had done so in part because I thought the Court would strike it down; now I came to feel that its safe passage through Congress would have been problematical at best.

At times, indeed, I wondered whether Congress was ready to pass any bill that provided for social insurance. Few of the influential members of the House and Senate were keen about social insurance, and many hated and feared it. (Seven years later, when I was in Congress, a representative from Ohio interrupted a speech I was making by shouting, "This social security is nothing but Godless communism!") I was thankful that the Committee on Economic Security had decided to leave health insurance out of the bill. Its inclusion would have aroused such vehement opposition, sparked by the American Medical Association, that the whole bill, even the simple grants to the states, would have gone down the drain.

I mentioned my fears about the impact of any health insurance to Miss Perkins. My advice wasn't needed; she and, I think, her committee colleagues had reached the same conclusion. It was ironic in a way, for the staff's strongest unit was the small group developing recommendations for health insurance. And it's a further irony that, again seven years later, I myself introduced a bill in Congress to establish a national system of health insurance—a bill drafted by a young man who had been Ed Witte's twenty-one-year-old assistant in 1934 and 1935 and who as Secretary of Health, Education, and Welfare thirty years later pushed the Medicare act through Congress: Wilbur J. Cohen.

In 1935 even sacrificing health insurance did not ensure passage of a bill that included other forms of social insurance. I insisted, therefore, that the bill should begin with "Title I: Grants to the States for Old Age Assistance." This was something everyone, Democrats and Republicans alike, could agree on. It wasn't a new or strange idea; it wasn't a great enhancement of federal power at the expense of the states; it was desperately needed; and it was undoubtedly constitutional. By leading off with it, the bill's proponents could count on a strongly favorable initial reaction in the Congress. In contrast, social insurance was a hard pill for many congressmen to swallow.

I've mentioned some of the troubles that unemployment insurance had in the Ways and Means Committee; what about old age insurance? Again, astonishingly, there was very little open, serious discussion of old age insurance. The Republicans opposed it, but didn't argue much. In the end, to the committee's formal report to the House (written by Witte and me) they filed a dissent, urging that old age insurance be stricken from the bill and made a subject of further study. Few Democrats were enthusiastic about it and many, including the most influential members, doubted its constitutionality. As I shared their doubts, it was a relief when, for an opinion, they turned not to me but to the Department of Justice.

Alexander Holtzoff—in his usual abrasive way—gave an hour's lecture to ten Democratic congressmen (and me), explaining why the bill was constitutional. Messrs. Doughton, Cooper, et al. were unconvinced. Finally they persuaded Assistant Solicitor General McLean to come up to Capitol Hill and give them *his* opinion. McLean was a courtly, white-haired Southerner, slow of speech and, I'm afraid, meagre in learning. He read a long statement, slowly and quietly. You could hear a pin drop. When he finished there were no questions (which was just as well) and the congressmen joined in a joyous expression of gratitude. Now they felt assured that the bill was constitutional. I successfully suppressed my laughter; I knew that every word that McLean read had been written by Holtzoff.

When in April the bill at long last came to the floor of the House, I was a wiser young man than I had been three months before—not a sadder one, to be sure, but thanks to Mr. Beaman a much humbler one. I was also exhausted. I took to my bed with a high fever; on arising, I went off to bask in the spring sunlight of the Great Smokies. So I missed the debate: missed the ovation for Davey Lewis, missed hearing Coya Knutson of Minnesota shout that I was "wet behind the ears" and Fred Vinson somewhat less accurately refer to me as the "able Assistant Secretary of Labor." I didn't witness the final clash, when the Republican minority voted almost solidly to strike out all provisions for old age insurance, or the anticlimactic roll call with its overwhelming majority in favor of the passage of the bill. Miss Perkins telegraphed me as soon as that roll call ended—a typical act of thoughtfulness by a great lady.

Then it was the Senate's turn. Several evenings I spent "rockin' on the po'ch," as I wrote home, with Senator Harrison and Leonard Calhoun. With his small pot belly, receding chin, and sleepy drawl, Harrison seemed a rather droll and lazy fellow; in reality he was keen, industrious, and determined. Calhoun, perhaps modeling himself on his chief, could also produce a misleading impression: he often described himself as just a poor country lawyer from Mississippi, but actually, before coming to Washington, he'd been in New York with a prestigious law firm.

On those warm spring nights the three of us went over the bill, page by page, as it had emerged from the House. The one thing that troubled me about it was, as usual, unemployment insurance. After the "leak" incident described above, the Ways and Means Committee failed to reinstate the provisions that allowed the extra credit for excused contributions. Ed Witte surmised that their failure to do so reflected a loss of confidence in the representatives of the Committee on Economic Security—in me, particularly, I suppose, because of that leak—but I doubt this. As I've mentioned, they did not seem to be angry with me, and they did not know of Altmeyer's involvement.

Fortunately, one member of the Senate Finance Committee was Robert M. LaFollette, Jr., of Wisconsin—a "small bubbling fountain of common sense," as Rebecca West called him in an essay describing a congressional hearing. Without much difficulty I drafted an amendment to the House bill, restoring the so-called merit rating provisions; in a lengthy telephone conversation I cleared my draft with Paul Raushenbush, making some changes that he suggested. I took the final version to Bob LaFollette, telling him, not too untruthfully, that this was Raushenbush's draft. LaFollette had no trouble in getting the Finance Committee to agree on this amendment.

Trouble, though, was what Witte foresaw as that committee went into executive session. He later observed that a very large percentage of the members of this committee were from south of the Mason-Dixon line and several were among the most conservative of all senators, and that to add to the difficulties, the United States Supreme Court on May 6 had held unconstitutional the Railroad Retirement Act. Language used in this decision seemed to apply to the old age insurance provisions of the social security bill. Once again, Assistant Solicitor General McLean was called on, to present his ghostwritten defense of the bill's constitutionality.

As a Perkins loyalist I did persuade Harrison, and he the committee, at least partially to reverse another House action. The original bill made the Department of Labor responsible for administering the whole program. The House, instead, placed administrative responsibility in an independent Social Security Board. Harrison agreed to put that board into the Department of Labor, provided, however, that the board, not the secretary, would have control over board personnel. The senator still resented the rebuff he had suffered, and while he agreed to this curious amendment I did not expect him to fight for it when the bill went to conference with the House representatives—and he didn't. The House version—an independent board—prevailed.

Attending the Finance Committee's executive session, I spent most of the time admiring Pat Harrison's political dexterity, as he won obviously reluctant support for one part of the bill after another; but I also was constantly watching one

Republican senator. This was Henry W. Keyes of New Hampshire, an aging gentlemen, the husband of a very popular novelist, Frances Parkinson Keyes, and an old college acquaintance of my father.

When I was home for a weekend in early May, my father said to me: "If I were a betting man, I would wager that in the committee meetings [which were about to begin] Harry Keyes will not say ten words." So I looked and listened. Each morning, the venerable senator, upon entering, smiled behind his moustache and bowed politely to one and all. Each time the committee was polled, instead of saying "aye" or "no" he nodded or shook his head. As far as one could tell, he had no more voice than a giraffe. Finally, the committee finished "reading the bill." Chairman Harrison embarked on a flowery oration of gratitude and praise for all and sundry—his colleagues, Mr. Beaman, the Senate draftsman, Leonard Calhoun, me, the president's committee. As he paused for breath, Senator Keyes looked up. Astonishingly, he opened his mouth; unbelievably, he *spoke*: "I move we adjourn."

Not all members of the Finance Committee had been silent during those executive sessions, and, for a change, there had been extended discussion of old age insurance. There was so much opposition to it, and so little overt support for it, that Ed Witte thought it would be stricken from the bill. Fortunately, he was very friendly with an outspoken opponent, Senator William Henry King of Utah. King asked him to prepare a statement against old age insurance for him (King) to deliver at a meeting of the Finance committee. Witte did so—and also prepared his own reply.

So after King made his speech, Chairman Harrison called on Witte to respond to it. He did so convincingly, point by point, demolishing all the arguments that he himself had prepared for Senator King. Harrison promptly welcomed a motion to strike out old age insurance; this motion was defeated by a substantial majority. Witte, Calhoun, and I privately agreed that if Harrison had allowed the question to be put prior to the King-Witte debate, old age insurance would have been deleted from the bill.

I looked forward eagerly to the Senate debate, for the Senate's rules (unlike those of the House) permitted non-members to be present on the floor, and Pat Harrison had invited both Calhoun and me to occupy chairs placed beside his front-row desk. The opening of debate was delayed for a day or two, because on June 12, 1935, Huey Long had embarked on a fifteen-hour speech that ended at four in the morning, and the senators took a day off to recover. On the fourteenth, before discussion of the Social Security bill began, Long again got the floor. He was soon interrupted by a point of "no quorum." While the roll was being called to see if a quorum was present, the Louisiana Kingfish strolled nonchalantly around the "well" of the Senate, between Harrison's desk and the vice president's rostrum. "Huey," said Harrison sleepily, "you talked long enough night before last. How long are you going to talk now?" "Five minutes, Senator, only five minutes more," was the earnest reply.

Three-quarters of an hour later, Long was again interrupted for a quorum call, and again he came pacing in front of us. Tipping back in his seat and keeping his eyes nearly closed, Harrison called to him: "Huey, I thought you said you were only going to talk five minutes." Long turned and answered solemnly: "That's right, Senator. I did say I'd talk five minutes. But it takes longer than that to make you understand!"

Harrison was still chuckling when the debate finally got under way. It was, on the whole, a relevant and statesmanlike discussion. The only fighting issue was raised by an amendment offered by Bennett Clark of Missouri that would have exempted from the old age insurance system those corporations that had instituted their own retirement benefit plans for their employees.

This amendment was, I think, the brainchild of a Philadelphian named Walter Forster. He had established a growing business of installing corporate retirement plans for the employees of various companies. Fearing that federal old age insurance would put an end to such plans, and to his business, Mr. Forster came to Washington and lobbied for an amendment that would exempt from the federal system employers who ran approved retirement plans for their own workers. He later told my father, who was a friend of his, that he spent $50,000 in this lobbying effort, I suppose in hotel bills, expensive food and drink for senators, and the printing and distribution of material describing and extolling various types of "Forster Plans." He got Senator Clark to introduce the amendment, and when the Finance Committee (by a tie vote) turned it down, Clark announced that he would propose and fight for it on the floor of the Senate.

This alarmed the Administration. What would become of all those actuarial predictions upon which the soundness of the federal scheme was based, if nobody could know or even guess how many companies, employing how many workers, would "opt out" of federal insurance? I found this question amusing, because I had an uninformed and probably unjustified suspicion of long-term actuarial predictions. Not amusing at all, however, was the danger that company plans would not in fact provide for workers in their old age. An employee might contribute for many years toward his retirement at sixty-five and then be fired and lose his pension rights when he was sixty-four. Mr. Forster's plans did not permit this, but in some then-existing corporate retirement schemes this had actually happened.

So destructive did the Clark Amendment seem that alarm bells rang in the White House. Tom Corcoran and Charles West, a former representative who had become Roosevelt's legislative liaison man, were told to join me in a lobbying effort against it. Each of us took four "doubtful" senators. The result of our efforts perhaps was an accurate measure of our skill or clout as lobbyists: Corcoran got all four of his men, I got two, and West none at all.

Actually, I thought I had the votes of three of my "targets" all signed up. The third man was Marcus Coolidge, senator from my own state of Massachusetts. Unable to find him—he was seldom on the floor or in his office—I got Senator David Walsh to promise to tell him to vote "No." When the Clark Amendment was nearing a vote, Walsh told me that Coolidge had got the message and had agreed to vote "No." Then the roll was called. "Mr. Coolidge?" "Aye." I walked over to Walsh with my eyebrows raised: he promptly whispered, "Ah, Tom, my colleague the junior senator from Massachusetts is a very strange man."* I got a laugh out of that, though the adoption of the Clark Amendment, by a sixteen-vote margin, was not a laughing matter. Still, I was cheerful; as I wrote on June 20, "I have chiefly been up at the Senate, running errands, giving advice, drafting amendments, and lobbying. Wandering about on the floor like a Senator was rather amusing."

A few days later I was still optimistic: "The bill has passed both houses all right, but the Senate put in a lot of amendments, some good, one very bad. So now there is a conference committee of five Representatives and five Senators, to see if they can compromise and agree. They cleared up most of the minor amendments Monday, the Senate 'receding' (giving up its amendment) in every case but one. The important ones will come up this afternoon." These "important ones" were the Clark Amendment and the LaFollette Amendment restoring the extra credit provision to the unemployment insurance section. The House had struck that out; now its conferees listened to an urgent demand by President Roosevelt and accepted the Senate version. They also heeded the president's warnings and adamantly opposed the Clark Amendment.

Senator Harrison invited Witte and me to attend the conference committee's sessions, but on one hot day "Senator King

---

*It was said of old Marcus Coolidge that when he ran for the Senate, his campaign assistants never allowed him to "ad lib" or make speeches of his own; he just read aloud what they wrote for him. When election day dawned, those assistants relaxed—too soon. That morning, without their knowledge, a radio station invited Coolidge to say a few words. He did so, and this is what he said: "This is election day. I urge all Democrats to vote, and to vote early and often."

had me and Witte ejected from the conference. So we sat in the air-cooled Senate and listened to Huey Long filibuster, and every five minutes were called into the conference to explain something. Childish procedure! King had no personal hard feelings; he talked to me at length afterwards, about his New England ancestors, but wanted to vote away from my gaze as a representative of the Administration." King quickly emerged as the strongest advocate, among the conferees, of the Clark Amendment. Mr. Forster had thoroughly convinced him.

After a while it even seemed possible that the whole bill would go down the drain, owing to the inability of the conferees to agree on whether to include the Clark Amendment. I wrote on August 1:

> It was very annoying when the conferees were all ready to agree on Tuesday, and instead of calling for a vote Pat Harrison palavered around so long that just as they *were* about to vote, Senator Clark, on King's invitation, came in and upset the applecart. Now, at Clark's request, the "experts," meaning a bunch of lobbyists and two other government men and me, are working very hard to reach a satisfactory compromise carrying out the purpose of Clark's amendment. It will take months—a silly hopeless job—but I've got to stick at it so that I'll be able to tell the conferees when they meet in ten days or so that I have tried my best and can't endorse a compromise draft without much more study. That'll be true enough.

I don't recall, now, which "lobbyists" I was referring to: presumably Mr. Forster, though he was no longer much in evidence. What I do remember is a long, hot stretch of hard labor, together with Leonard Calhoun and a St. Louis lawyer named William Woodward, whom Clark enlisted presumably because he was counsel for Socony Vacuum, a corporation that had installed one of the Forster retirement plans. We had to redraft the amendment, closing every imaginable loophole so that the employees' rights would be protected, and we had to assess what effect the exemption of companies with retirement plans would have on the financial aspects of the bill—the rates of taxation and the amount of benefits. This required a vast amount of actuarial calculation, and for once I blessed the actuaries who I think were in the Treasury Department. After a week they threw up their hands; it would take them weeks, maybe months, to come up with figures that made sense. At the same time, Woodward agreed with Calhoun and me that we, too, needed more time to complete our task.

We had been, as I wrote home,

> working day and night through bad heat. . . . The idea was that Clark would fight any killing of his Amendment unless it was clearly demonstrated that no substitute could be worked out in ten days. So, to prevent anyone from saying that *I* had prevented the substitute from being completed, I had to work especially hard. Finally I got Clark's own attorney to join me [and Calhoun] in signing a statement to the effect that the job couldn't be done till September at the earliest. I read this statement to the conferees and the Senate at last receded and dropped the Clark [amendment]. So now the President has the bill.

And at that point I was happy about that bill. Especially, of course, about its unemployment insurance sections—partly because by then I had come to think of them as mine, and partly because Mr. Justice Brandeis would approve of them. The welfare provisions—the grants to the states for assistance to the needy—were certainly helpful, not only in terms of the state treasuries and the destitute recipients of aid. They—especially the grants for old age assistance—were political assets. Pat Harrison once told me that the best thing I had done was to make "Grants to the States for Old Age Assistance" the first chapter of the bill, for that was what evoked an immediate favorable response on Capitol Hill. And that's exactly why I *had* placed it first!

As for old age insurance, I still had doubts about its constitutionality, and regretted the absence of "government contributions" and the consequent high rate of the regressive tax on wages (the employee half of the payroll tax); but it was an awful lot better than nothing, and did put a quietus on such movements as the Townsend Plan. Furthermore, it could be amended to rectify what I thought were its chief shortcomings—as, indeed, it was in 1939.

On August 14, at a ceremony in the oval office, the president signed the bill. I wasn't there. In the group photograph taken on that occasion, Roosevelt is fittingly flanked by Senator Wagner and Representative Lewis—and all three of them are beaming. Soberly, right behind the president's chair, stands Miss Perkins. That was as it should be—but next to her is—of all people—the aforementioned Senator King of Utah! What was *he* doing there? After the picture was taken and the bill was signed, Miss Perkins gave a copy of it to the president, who autographed it for me, "with thanks to Tom Eliot." A framed copy of the bill's first and last pages, surrounding a picture of the president and Miss Perkins together, has been on my wall ever since.

I was not a bit disappointed by not being invited to the White House ceremony. I was enjoying a party with my peers on an outdoor terrace, with music and dancing. I found myself dancing with a girl with whom I had a slight acquaintance, a very proper and, I thought, serious-minded young lady. Suddenly, for no reason I could ascertain—possibly I was being just too smug and stuffy—she reached out and gave my necktie a hard yank. Exactly a year later, our engagement was announced.

Chapter 6

The Social Security Board

SKIPPER wants to know if Lincoln would prefer Witt or Witte." That was the cable I sent to Charlie Wyzanski in Geneva, where he was attending a meeting of the International Labor Organization. I sent it, at Miss Perkins's request, shortly after the Senate had passed both the National Labor Relations bill and the Social Security bill.

Earlier, I had sent another mysterious cable to Charlie, informing him of the Supreme Court's decision in the NRA case; for that one, we had a prearranged code, wherein, for instance, "Alabama" meant "undue delegation of power," "Arizona" meant "not interstate commerce," and so on. But in sending the later message, I decided, correctly, that Wyzanski could easily figure it out without any previous agreement on a code. "Skipper" surely meant Roosevelt. "Lincoln"—I thought this was just a bit risky, but Charlie grasped it immediately— was John Gilbert Winant, the ex-governor of New Hampshire who had become assistant director of the I.L.O. People had often remarked on his "Lincolnian looks." "Witt" was the labor lawyer, Nat Witt, on the staff of the Labor Board. And "Witte," of course, was my friend Ed, the expert on welfare and social insurance.

Wyzanski deciphered the message: would Winant prefer to be chairman of the National Labor Relations Board or the Social Security Board? He cabled two words in reply. "Ed Witte." Accordingly, soon after the signing of the Social Security Act, the president appointed Winant chairman of the Social Security Board. The other two members were Altmeyer and an Arkansas lawyer, Vincent Miles.

Through most of the long struggle to get the bill enacted I had given little thought to my own future. Congressman Treadway had roared genially that I should be chairman of the Social Security Board, which was laughable nonsense—although, much later, Calhoun told me that Senator Harrison had recommended me for membership on the board. It was Calhoun who alerted me to a more imaginable possibility—nay, probability—when one day in late July he drawled, "Tom, when you're general counsel of this new board, I'd like to be one of your assistants." (He was.)

Later that day I drove to an outdoor cocktail party, my mind spinning with the wheels. I had just turned twenty-eight; could I conceivably handle this assignment? I had learned a lot, but I was still too young. Nevertheless, maybe—yes, I could swing it *if* I could have at my right hand an older man, a steadying influence, a person of wide experience and mature judgment. Leonard Calhoun didn't fill the bill, for he was just my age.

No sooner had I arrived at my destination than I saw among the guests, at the far corner of the terrace, a man named Jack Tate, a lawyer who'd been in the State Department and then in the NRA. I didn't know him very well, but I knew, instantly, that he was the older man I needed. I walked over to him and said abruptly: "Jack, if I'm made general counsel of the Social Security Board, will you be my first assistant?" He looked at me calmly for a few seconds, smiled slightly, and answered, "Yes." He was thirty-two years old.

Officially, the board did not take office until October 1, and soon after the bill's enactment I entrained for a brief holiday at my family's summer home in Maine. In the dining car I was seated opposite two much older men, who, I thought, didn't know me from a hole in the ground, though I recognized one of them as a wealthy summer resident of Northeast Harbor and head of the yachting fleet there. Ignoring me, they talked at each other, each trying to outdo the other in denouncing Roosevelt. Then to my delight the yachting fleet man, not looking at me, said, "But there's one thing even worse than Franklin Roosevelt, and that's a federal bureaucrat." I spent the rest of the meal looking impassive and wondering if he knew who I was. I never did find out.

Returning, refreshed, to Washington, I found that everything was slowed up because of the antics of Huey Long. On the final night of that session of Congress, after a fixed time for adjournment had been agreed upon, the bill appropriating funds for the Social Security Board was one of the measures still awaiting final Senate action. There was no controversy about it; it simply needed to be put to a vote. But before it was, Long took the floor and spoke—about anti-Southern discrimination in the economic system, I think—for hour after hour. So the time for adjournment arrived and no money had been appropriated for the Social Security Board.

The duties prescribed by the act had to be performed somehow, with or without appropriations. Money could be shifted from unused accounts and, especially, personnel could be borrowed from, and paid by, the NRA. That very large organization had been spinning its wheels ever since its chief functions had been held unconstitutional in May, and it had a lot of mostly idle employees and unspent money. It was from there that I planned to snatch Jack Tate—if I got the general counsel's job, which would be a board appointment.

I wrote on September 6 after returning from my vacation,

Here the situation is interesting. It appears that Miss Perkins cabled Winant at length about me and he cabled back that he would be "delighted." Altmeyer assumes that I will be general counsel and has had several consultations with me as if I were. Miles, however, has not been approached and will arrive Monday. Meanwhile, I am seeing a steady stream of applicants—some amusing, some pathetic, a few promising. I have been blessing Huey Long because I can tell each applicant that his chances are virtually *nil* because Long kept the Board from getting sufficient funds! . . . Middle-aged Southerners predominate. . . . If I get the job my two first assistants would be from Tennessee [Tate] and Mississippi [Calhoun], so that ought to satisfy the Southern delegation.

(Two days later the man whom I'd been "blessing," Huey Long, was assassinated in Baton Rouge.)

I got the job only after Winant had prudently looked me over at a protracted luncheon, and had got good reports about me from Capitol Hill. Vincent Miles was another matter. Fortunately for me, he knew and admired my brother Charles. But he didn't know me and at first seemed hostile.

> Mr. Miles called me in, showed irritation at Winant having committed himself to me in advance, and asked if I was just going to stay on the job a year and then go into a lucrative practice or run for Congress! I quite truthfully said I didn't care for private practice and far from running for Congress didn't even know what part of the country I wanted to locate in. Next day he was much pleasanter and called my appointment "official." It's not, and won't be till sometime next week, but I am working as such already and have borrowed four NRA lawyers to help. I don't know how much Miles will try to influence my appointments. He's one of these guys who is indirect, and hints and insinuates; but I've seen enough of Southern pols to guess pretty well what they mean. (Doesn't seem to be gentlemanly, or something, to say right out what you mean.)

As I reread this letter more than fifty-five years later, I have to smile and shake my head; Vint Miles never did pressure me into appointing particular individuals, and that question he asked me was certainly shrewd!

Soon I was writing: "I've worked three of the last four nights. Lots of things happening: and aside from about four others, our legal staff does it all. . . . It is rather embarrassing, to get positive directions on some point of policy from one Board member and exactly the opposite instructions from another. The big differences are Altmeyer v. Winant (speed and non-legal attitude v. great care and caution) and Miles v. Winant (politicos and older lawyers v. nonpolitical young lawyers)."

In both of these intra-board differences of opinions I was strongly on the side of Winant. The Social Security Act was an experiment. Yes, it had passed both houses by large majorities—but before it did so, nearly every Republican representative had voted to kill old age insurance, and a majority of senators had been willing to gouge and distort that program. I felt that a great number of hostile critics were just waiting, ready to pounce if the board made a single mistake, and that it was my job to see that the board adhered strictly to the law. This made Altmeyer angry: it wasn't that he wanted to break the law; he just wanted to get things done in a hurry.

As for the lawyers whom I should recruit, as I've said, Miles did not foist any deadbeats on me despite his preference for "older lawyers"; ironically, it was Altmeyer who insisted that I needed a wise, old legal adviser and persuaded me to employ a clientless Florida attorney who had a magnificent mane of white hair, was frequently effusive in expressing gratitude for his appointment, and sent me and my wife Christmas crates of oranges long after our paths diverged.

Beyond question, I needed a large and able staff. The Department of Justice, of course, would handle the defense of the federal statute in the courts, but we could foresee cases testing the validity of various state laws, in which we would be asked to help. Right from the start, we were being asked to advise state legislatures to draft bills that would comply with the standards set by the Social Security Act—mostly unemployment compensation bills. An endless series of questions as to coverage had to be answered, often after granting a hearing to the person who thought he wouldn't have to pay the payroll tax or the one who wanted to be sure that he would be entitled to old age benefits. And as the board began to gear up for one of the biggest administrative jobs in history—the efficient and accurate keeping of tax and benefit payment records for millions of people—our attorneys became deeply involved in conventional legal work, negotiating and drafting contracts with suppliers of materials, the largest being IBM. Today's computers were still just a dream, but business machines were real and, in our eyes in those long-ago days, amazing.

My own job had several different aspects. First, I felt it was my duty to keep the board on the straight and narrow path. This was not an easy task. Altmeyer's annoyance with lawyers in general finally was focused squarely on me. We had never got along comfortably together; now, for a while, as he perceived me to be an obstructive and cocksure nay-sayer, our relationship deteriorated. My letters during the first year of the board's existence are only too full of complaints about "insults that grow tiresome." But as time passed the tension eased; when Winant went away for a month, his "absence has made a changed man of Altmeyer, who actually sends his letters up for our o.k. before he sends 'em out." And later I described Altmeyer as "definitely valuable as a Board member."

The board, once it got going, met frequently, and on Miles's motion voted to have me present. After a couple of months I was writing: "The Board is very deliberate, with Altmeyer heedless of the danger of making bad precedents, and Miles unwilling to do anything rash or possibly questionable, and Winant silent between them. I am getting more used to them and begin to find Board meetings less exhausting." That same letter suggests that I was not "exhausted" at all: "Dancing was lots of fun last Wednesday night. . . . Last night dinner at [Washington Post editor] Felix Morley's was amusing: five lawyers present, two (John Dickinson and I) New Dealers, two (Jouett Shouse and Dean Acheson) Democrats bitterly against F. D.; and one, Emory Niles of Baltimore, on the fence. Felix Morley played *enfant terrible.*"

Only once, in my records and my memory, is there any case of the board's taking imprudent action, though one letter does mysteriously mention "chickens coming home to roost." What I do clearly recall is what occurred six or seven years later, after I had been elected to Congress, involving Altmeyer, me, and the Social Security Board. The last (dominated by Altmeyer, who was already beginning to be called "Mr. Social Security") had found that the State of Ohio had flouted the standards prescribed by the act and the rules and regulations of the board in the administration of its old age assistance program. After giving the state due warning, the board stopped making grants to Ohio.

As I recall it, the abuses had been glaring, with pensions recorded as having been allegedly paid to many people long since dead. The board was certainly justified in insisting that drastic changes be made before it would renew the grants. But some Ohio politicians sought to tear to pieces the whole notion of enforceable federal standards. They caused a bill to be introduced in Congress, directing the board to make the grant. This bill was referred to the Judiciary Committee of the House. I was a member of that committee. I telephoned James Rowe at the White House, who told me that he was sure that the president would veto this bill if Altmeyer thought it was important to do so. I then called Altmeyer. We agreed, heartily, on the importance of defeating that bill. I am glad that in my last contact with him we were standing together, and that I was able to bury, in committee, a measure of which we both so strongly disapproved.

By 1936 my own bill-drafting days were pretty well over, but not entirely. State legislatures, wishing to take quick advantage of the act's tax-offset provisions and "keep the money at home," were glad to have help in drafting unemployment compensation bills. Those bills were drafted by the highly competent section of my staff assigned to that subject: seven lawyers, each under thirty, from seven different law schools, where each had been editor of the law review. I did work with them in preparing an *amicus curiae* brief when the validity of the Washington state law was attacked, but I confined my bill-drafting efforts to fulfilling the pledge made to the conference committee to produce an acceptable version of the Clark Amendment. Bill Woodward came on from St. Louis, and he and Calhoun and I resumed our labors. Eventually I notified Senator Harrison that we were ready.

Harrison appointed a joint committee, naming Senator King as chairman, and King called a meeting on the evening of March 30, 1936. He and Clark were the only senators in attendance; four representatives, including Chairman Doughton of Ways and Means, were present. So were Murray Latimer, head of the Social Security Board's old age benefits division,* and, of course, Mr. Forster of Philadelphia. Let the record state what transpired:

> SENATOR KING: Shall we proceed? Mr. Doughton, what are your views as to how we shall proceed? Shall we hear from the experts?
>
> MR. DOUGHTON: I suppose that is proper; I suppose that is the first thing to do.
>
> SENATOR KING: Mr. Eliot, have you any report to make?

So there I was, an expert, no less! But the tone of the statement (or "report") that I then made was less assertive than usual.

> Mr. Calhoun and I have tried to carry out our promise to this committee. We have taken part in the work of seeing whether legislation encouraging private pension systems can be so framed that adequate protection is given not only to the employers with such systems, but to their employees and the government as well. There has been prepared, largely by Mr. Woodward, a draft of proposed legislation for encouraging private pension systems. We . . . worked with the common objective of furnishing your committee with the safest and most practical legislation the problem permits. . . . I feel great hesitancy in stating that the draft which will be presented will accomplish its intended purpose. I do feel, however, that it more nearly accomplishes the objectives of the committee than does any legislation previously suggested. . . . In concluding I feel it proper to mention that my inexpertness in the field of insurance may have resulted in my being unaware of many difficulties inherent in this proposed amendment. I do feel, however, that the draft which will be presented is less objectionable than any previously considered.

They questioned me, and I kept up my modest demeanor. Doughton disliked my phrase "less objectionable." "Do you want us to understand," he asked crossly, "that it is objectionable but not seriously objectionable?" "Well," I conceded, " 'objectionable' perhaps is an unfortunate word. To this draft ob-

---

*This division was so named in order to avoid any mention of "insurance"; the more we could speak of "benefits" without mentioning payroll taxes, the better—at least until the Supreme Court decided the constitutional question.

jections would be made." Senator Clark promptly tried to get a rise out of me: "*Of course* objections would be made to *any* scheme proposed. . . . Very serious objections can probably be made to the act itself; it goes into effect but is made legal ultimately by the Supreme Court of the United States. Any scheme that anyone may devise, particularly in a new field such as this, may be subject to objections." This was said in a challenging tone, but I did not argue; I just said, "I agree with you."

Bill Woodward "presented" the bill simply by handing copies around and spending ten minutes explaining it. At nine o'clock the committee adjourned, agreeing to meet again on the following Saturday morning. Early Saturday I drove to the Hill and found King in his office. He was surprised by my arrival. "Why are you here?" he asked. I said I wanted to speak with him before the meeting. "Oh," he laughed, "the meeting's been called off. Mr. Forster was in to see me yesterday. You know, last summer he was afraid the new law would ruin his business. But now he tells me that the new law's got everyone thinking about old age pensions and retirement schemes, and his business has just been growing and growing. So now he doesn't want any Clark Amendment and neither do I, so you can forget it!"*

Often, when not attending board meetings or doing a little bill drafting or brief writing, I was out of town, engaged in a third phase of my job: education. Again I stress the novelty of social insurance in 1935. Responsible state officials began asking for advice before that year was out. In 1936 the demand for information became more widespread. The payroll tax for old age insurance would begin to be imposed in January 1937. What would that whole system mean to the average individual? Would he have to wear around his neck a kind of license plate

---

*One curious thing about this episode is that while I recall my conversation with Senator King clearly enough, I have no recollection of the hearing or even of working again with Calhoun and Woodward on the new draft. Nor was there any mention of these matters in my letters. The record of the hearing was brought to my attention in 1986 by Ms. Lupu of Harvard's Kennedy School of Government.

with his number on it? This was one of the far-out pictures dreamed up by some Republican campaigners in the election of 1936. Alf Landon, the G.O.P. candidate for president, mistakenly (and uncharacteristically) attacked the social security program; the attack backfired, and it did leave many people worried or at least curious.

Why I should have been the Social Security Board's traveling teacher I don't know. Perhaps the board members and Frank Bane, the kindly Virginian who became the board's executive director, were just too busy, and certainly Winant and Altmeyer disliked speech making. In contrast, I enjoyed it. So I had only just become general counsel when I hit the road, right after moving into my third and last bachelor household: "We had a tremendous party here Saturday, from five till after eleven—close to two hundred guests, many of whom apparently forgot their suppers. It was a crowded but genial occasion, a housewarming for fair. I go to speak to Rotary at Hagerstown on Wednesday; to the shipbuilders and shippers in New York on Friday; to the retailers of Pittsburgh the following Thursday; and to the certified public accountants of North Carolina at Winston Salem the following day, Friday, if I can get there." During that same autumn of 1935 I traveled to private conferences, too, with state officials in New Jersey and Illinois, and at Raleigh "with the crafty Governor and stupid Atty. Gen. of North Carolina."

A full year later, after the presidential election, I felt that I was almost on the campaign trail myself. The old age insurance program was about to begin. This was the time for both explication and reassurance. With my bride of seven weeks I made a "swing around the circle"—St.Louis, Des Moines, St. Paul, Minneapolis, Cleveland. "We left Tuesday night and got to St. Louis at noon the next day." All our journeys, of course, were by train. "Speech to about 250 under auspices of the League of Women Voters . . . and . . . appointments all Thursday, mostly with the Governor's Social Security Commission. Then, night train to Des Moines, clear and cool, an attractive city, also a thriving one. Many calls and conferences with State and party [?] officials. There was a good meeting of the Chamber of Commerce, at lunch, with 350 there, and a very responsive audience too—fun to talk to. Some very nice ladies picked up Lois and took her all around the town and even sent her flowers."

During a sociable weekend in St. Paul, where we both had several friends—and where the temperature hit 18° below—I had conferences with "officials from both Dakotas as well as Minnesota" and made one brief speech. Then, "Monday noon was the gala event of the trip, lunch in Minneapolis with the combined Minneapolis and St. Paul Civic and Commerce Ass'ns., approximately 1000 present. Also the Governor and both Mayors and the Chief Justice.They were all introduced and rose, and then Lois had to get up too. I had to holler, but the speech was all right I guess. Anyway it had the effect of changing the Governor's mind. Monday morning he had announced that he wouldn't call a special session of the legislature to pass unemployment insurance—and now he's called it!"

After that, and a long day on the train, Cleveland might have been an anticlimax, but if so it wasn't a bad one. "Another fine C of C meeting, (450 paid); then a 15-minute radio speech at five o'clock, then a talk at a Consumers' League supper. Then we staggered into our last Pullman." There was still one speech to be made, though: not on the campaign trail but in Washington to a nationwide audience, for I was scheduled for a Sunday afternoon radio talk over a national network. And now not Cleveland but I myself turned out to be the anticlimax. Arriving at the radio station ahead of time, I listened to the broadcast that would immediately precede my own. And what was it? It was King Edward VIII, "now at long last" announcing his abdication from the throne of Great Britain and his preference for "the woman I love." After that, when I gave my talk, can't you just see millions of eager Americans listening to me pontificate about old age insurance?

So much for speech making, which I enjoyed; now let me turn back to personnel administration, which I didn't. At least I often complained, in my letters, that it was occasionally disheartening and always unduly time-consuming. Yet there were things about it that I remember with pride and pleasure, and incidents that still make me smile when I think of them.

My chief pride was in the caliber not only of my top staff people, Tate, Calhoun, and later Alan Wilcox and Robert Bingham, but of that small, elite section that concentrated on unemployment compensation. All seven young lawyers in that section were stars. Brightest among them was Bernice Lotwin, one of the first people we "borrowed" from the NRA. She did a lot of field work; state legislators, at first highly skeptical of a twenty-eight-year-old woman lawyer, were soon impressed by her knowledge and the wise advice she gave them and captivated by her charm. (Later, after she married Bernard Bernstein, she made social security her career, serving for many years as regional attorney in New York.) Another member of that section who had a distinguished career was G. Mennen "Soapy" Williams, thrice governor of Michigan and thereafter a justice of that state's Supreme Court. Bernice Lotwin we'd borrowed; "Soapy" came looking for a job and got it immediately—who was I to sniff at a Princeton Phi Beta Kappa and an editor of the University of Michigan Law Review?

Several of the others I'd met, or they had been highly recommended, and I just picked up the phone to start recruiting them. As far as I can recall, the only person who turned me down—he preferred to go into teaching—was a new Yale Law graduate named Edward H. Levi. Thirty years later, when I was a university president and the campuses were in a revolutionary uproar, Ed Levi's performance as president of the University of Chicago won my unstinted respect.

Another member of that unemployment section was Edwin R. Teple. Like Williams, he was a big, rangy fellow; unlike Williams, he seemed shy and humble, and in aspect rough-hewn. He told me he'd just graduated from Ohio State Law School. "Top of the class, I suppose," I said with a grin. He sadly shook his head. "No. No. That is, I was second." "Too bad," I said. "What happened? Were you on the law review?" Nodding apologetically, he replied: "I was editor-in-chief. But that wasn't the trouble. I took on another job. The American Law Institute got me to prepare a restatement of the law of torts; it took a lot of time. I shouldn't have done it."

It did not take me any time to tell him that I was much interested in his application and would have the board's personnel director check his references; was he staying on in Washington? Yes, until the matter was settled. "Where can I reach you by phone?" He paused and shook his head: "Nowhere. I'm staying in my pup tent, down by the river."

Needless to say, he got the job, and I think it was just after he did so that he married Roberta, his high school sweetheart. A few months later, when he was on an assignment away from Washington, it was my turn to get married. On my wedding morning came a letter from Ed Teple. I haven't kept it but remember it well. It went roughly like this: "Congratulations! Wish Roberta and I could be at your wedding, and we're sure you'll be as happy as we've been. And we *are* happy even though we can't afford all the comforts we'd really like; I expect, Tom, that you, like me, will find that it's just not true that two can live as cheaply as one. And you'll think you're the luckiest guy in the world to have Lois as your wife, just as I think, even though it's hard to make ends meet, that I'm the luckiest guy because I've got Roberta. . . ." Needless to say, he got the raise!

Aside from Bernice Lotwin, no member of the unemployment compensation section was originally borrowed from the NRA. I did acquire some good lawyers in that borrowing process, among them Peter Seitz, later famous as the arbitrator who put an end to professional baseball's "reserve clause." But not all the NRA people were satisfactory. I could get rid of them fairly painlessly, for they could go back to the NRA and work there (doing what, I have no idea) until the money ran out a year or so later.

However, one of them did not want to go back. A few days

after he and three others joined my staff and were given desks in a single office—for space was at a premium—the three other men came to me saying that they'd quit if I didn't get rid of their office-mate. The three were competent, promising people; the fourth, a South Carolinian whom I shall call Marshy, was not. The real trouble was that from morning to night Marshy never stopped talking, and the other three couldn't get any work done. Eventually, I told Marshy to go back to the NRA. Early the next morning I received an angry telephone call from the secretary (now the title is "Executive Assistant") of Senator James M. Byrnes of South Carolina. He demanded that I reinstate Marshy. I said I really couldn't, and that I'd like to explain why to the senator, but not over the telephone. The secretary said, in a menacing tone, "Oh, you'll be hearing from the senator all right." I did indeed. In the late afternoon, Senator Byrnes called me: "It's about Mr. Marshy, Mr. Eliot. He's been here all day, and I just want you to know that I quite understand why you must get rid of him!"

Another NRA lawyer, or rather a *former* NRA lawyer, whom I didn't borrow and who applied for a job, came armed with a strong letter of recommendation from Mrs. Roosevelt. He was a pleasant gentleman in his fifties, a part-time farmer, a very minor poet, and a person with some experience in welfare administration. I asked him why he had left the NRA. "Why," he said excitedly, "do you know what they did to me? They put me under some young hotshot young enough to be my son!" When I let out a roar of laughter he stared at me at first in puzzlement and then in horror. Because of his sponsor, I hired him.

I think that that was the only time that I was pressured by the White House, in any way, to make particular appointments. But I did see how the recruiting of a large staff could be turned into a political asset for the board. A judicious use of patronage could gain or cement the favorable opinion of key members of Congress. Some of the latter asked me to appoint their constituents, and didn't seem to mind when, as sometimes happened,

I had to say, "No, not that gentleman; please recommend someone who has such-and-such qualifications and I'll gladly appoint him." Sometimes I went out of my way to solicit recommendations from such influential congressmen as Fred Vinson and Jere Cooper. Almost all these patronage appointees turned out satisfactorily. The brilliant young man whom I recruited to be our regional attorney in New York, Walter Gellhorn, threatened to resign when I named as his assistant a man recommended by Representative John Boylan, a typical Tammany politician who chaired the Appropriations Subcommittee that handled the Social Security Board's budget. A few months later, Walter was full of praise for his assistant.

A few members of Congress who had no close connection with social security legislation tried to place needy constituents on my staff. I remember two of them, Representative Benjamin Whelchel of Georgia and Senator Robert Reynolds of North Carolina.

Whelchel gave me a bad scare. He telephoned for an appointment and I said I'd see him (and his constituent) at eleven-thirty. At eleven-twenty I was summoned to attend an emergency board meeting. It was too late to stop the congressman from coming; I just had to ask Calhoun to handle the matter. An hour later, when I got back from the meeting, Calhoun met me with a grave face and handed me an envelope. In it was a short, handwritten letter from the congressman, telling me what a heel I was to have stood him up and declaring his intention to denounce me, and the Social Security Board, on the floor of the House. I ran to my car and whizzed up to Capitol Hill.

Luck was with me. In the corridor outside the House chamber, I saw a friendly member of the Ways and Means Committee, Wesley Disney of Oklahoma. I asked him if he'd go into the Chamber, find Whelchel, and bring him out to me. He did so. Whelchel shook hands politely enough, looking surprised. The surprise was mingled with pleasure when I said: "I wonder if I've seen you before. Did you play guard on the Georgia team that beat Harvard about fifteen years ago? I watched that game." He stared at me and then began to grin. "No, that was my cousin, Puss Whelchel." I concluded this colloquy by nodding and saying, "He was All-American." We chatted amiably, and the threat of denunciation was forgotten.

The most persistent senator was Reynolds. Three times he appeared in my office with his arm around the shoulders of an unhappy and unqualified constituent, a different man each time, and said: "Mr. Eliot, I want you to meet the best damn lawyer in North Ca'lina." Before he could do this a fourth time, I went up to the Hill and was shown into his office. He was talking with a distinguished banker from Winston-Salem, but took time out to listen to my explanation as to why I had not appointed any of his people. He then thanked me warmly, and said to the banker: "This is a fine young man. He's the *only* man in this administration, suh, who's had the courtesy to come up here and talk with me!"

I rather prided myself, justifiably I think, on my success at the patronage game. Arthur Altmeyer realized this. His attitude toward me, while no longer antagonistic, was at least combative, and he decided to play at patronage himself. After a trip to his home state of Wisconsin he told me that he had recruited a fine Milwaukee lawyer for my staff, a man with a great Democratic Party record. I swallowed hard, said okay, and wondered what to do about it; I couldn't have individual board members appointing my lawyers.

I didn't have long to wonder. Soon came a telephone call from the loyal New Deal congressman from Milwaukee, Tom O'Malley. He nearly deafened me. "What the hell do you mean," he shouted, "by giving a job to that son-of-a-bitch who ran against me in the last primary and slandered me and Roosevelt?" I told him what had happened. I assume that he then gave Altmeyer an earful; anyway, that Milwaukee lawyer never showed up, and from then on, no Social Security Board appointments could be made without an investigation by the board's personnel office and the approval of its director, Henry Aronson.

Eventually the board got its appropriation from Congress, but more difficulties were ahead. To the next year's budget was added an amendment proposed by the acerbic old senator from Virginia, Carter Glass. He had been enraged because someone he had recommended had not been appointed and because the board's regional office had been placed in Roanoke instead of his home town, Lynchburg. His amendment (as well as his wrath) was aimed at his fellow Virginian Frank Bane; it provided that no salary should be paid to any high-ranking officer of the board until that person had been nominated by the president and the nomination had been confirmed by the Senate.

The president promptly nominated Bane, the several bureau chiefs affected, and me—but the nominations were then sent to a Senate committee of which Glass was chairman. He refused to call a meeting of his committee to act on them so that they could go before the full Senate. Soon he went home to Lynchburg, to be with his dying wife, taking the nomination documents with him. She died; he returned and finally—after we had had a couple of payless paydays—he called his committee together and recommended our names to the Senate. Frank Bane told me, with tears in his eyes, that on her deathbed Mrs. Glass had whispered to her husband: "Don't be mean to Frank Bane."

Late on the afternoon before the Senate was to vote on the confirmation of the president's nominees, I went off to play tennis. To the tennis court came a friend, a reporter on the *Boston Herald* named Henry Ehrlich. He told me that he had just learned from Senator Lodge of Massachusetts that my nomination would be strongly opposed by Senator Joseph Guffey of Pennsylvania.

I was astonished. I had never met Senator Guffey. What would the objection be based on? Maybe he would say that I and my staff were much too young, that only a few favored states were represented on the staff, that only Ivy League law school graduates had been employed. I wrote a very brief memorandum covering these three points, and next morning took it to my old friend Senator Walsh. I told him that Guffey was going to object to my confirmation that afternoon, and that I didn't know why. Walsh said he'd be ready to speak on my behalf if necessary.

When I got back to my office I was told to call Henry Aronson, the personnel director. "Good news finally," Aronson said. "There were some questions about Reitman and it's taken us a month to clear them up, but everything's all right and you can go ahead." "Reitman?" I said. "Yes." "Reitman? What are you talking about, Henry?" "Why, your candidate for the regional attorneyship in Pennsylvania—Reitman." A great light dawned. I thanked Aronson and telephoned Guffey's office. To the secretary who answered I said, enthusiastically, "Please tell the senator that I'm just delighted because Mr. Reitman's appointment has been cleared and I trust he'll be ready to start work next week."

In the Senate a few hours later, my name was read for confirmation. Up rose Senator Guffey: "This is a fine young man, the grandson of a great educator and himself a very able lawyer. I strongly support his confirmation." And I still chuckle when I recall what happened next. Apropos of nothing that had been mentioned, Senator Walsh spoke up: "The office of the General Counsel of the Social Security Board consists of ninety lawyers whose average age is thirty-eight, who come from thirty-nine different states, and are graduates of twenty-five different law schools."

Whether they were law review editors or ward heelers, all the Social Security Board lawyers were members of *my staff*. An important part of my job, as I saw it, was to have the members of that staff be both productive and happy. On the whole, I think they were. Of course there were moments of tension and disaffection—once, a young attorney who hadn't had a raise in salary brought a gun to the office, whether to shoot me or himself I never learned—but, overall, morale was high. In maintaining it, Jack Tate and Leonard Calhoun were invaluable. I contributed something by organizing a softball team. Nobody had to play but many were glad to, and others came to cheer at our after-hours or weekend contests. As I wrote: "Lots of fun this morning [April 11,1937] playing baseball [*sic*]. I've organized a General Counsel's office team. We lost to the mimeographers today, but should improve with practice!" We didn't; but we did manage to defeat our keenest rival, the Bureau of Unemployment Compensation. In that game, playing first base and batting cleanup, I hit a home run. Thereafter, I couldn't hit at all, and by late July had placed myself at the eighth spot in the batting order.

My own morale, shaky in the early months at the board, improved astronomically in the summer and fall of 1936, when I got engaged and married. By Christmas of that year I was writing home:

> The best thing was yesterday when Winant gave me—and our office—an unexpected and grand boost. Getting married seems to have improved my good humor, and apparently one is judged by one's humor! Well, it was encouraging anyway. I seem to be on fine terms with everyone in authority. . . . I am happy about the States passing unemployment compensation laws. Many of those laws will cease if Title IX of our Act is thrown out by the Supreme Court; but N.Y., Wisconsin, and now Penna. and Maryland and N.C. and maybe several more are passing laws clearly designed to be permanent. I think the program is justified and the [Wagner-Lewis] method vindicated, whatever the Court does. The old age benefits program is vaster. I have never been wholly sold on it: more of the money for it should come from graduated income taxes. F.D. was wrong on the huge reserve, as everybody but Morgenthau told him. Well, there's plenty of time to fix it.

Curiously, the shadow of uncertainty as to the law's validity did not seem to dishearten me or my colleagues. As expected, early in 1936 the Supreme Court did declare the Agricultural Adjustment Act unconstitutional, and the applicability of its decision to our old age benefit program was obvious. But in the winter of 1937, just as I was beginning to meet with Wyzanski and Robert Jackson* to prepare the arguments in favor

---

*Wyzanski had moved to the Justice Department; Jackson was assistant attorney-general.

of our Act, a new factor complicated the situation. That was Roosevelt's "Court-packing plan"—his proposal to add up to six justices to the Supreme Court. Wyzanski was bitterly but quietly opposed to the plan. I also kept quiet about it, even in my private letters. A year earlier, I had not been quite so circumspect in a letter beginning "Now comes the news of the disgraceful AAA decision. . . . The Court has lined up utterly with 'the forces of entrenched greed,' and at last I agree we need either a new court, a constitutional amendment, or, preferably, a court so limited that, in Stone's language, it cannot usurp the legislative power. These autocrats . . . must have their whiskers trimmed."

Was Roosevelt's Court-packing plan the whisker-trimming that I wished for? I don't suppose that anyone will ever know for sure whether that plan really caused Chief Justice Hughes and Justice Roberts to break with the "battalion of death" and join forces with their liberal colleagues, Brandeis, Cardozo, and Stone. Nor can anyone say positively that the Court-packing bill would have been enacted if the Court had struck down the National Labor Relations Act and the Social Security Act, the subjects of the major cases it had to decide while the debate on Capitol Hill was raging. I did have the perspicacity to write that if those two statutes were upheld by the Court, the plan would be defeated—which is what happened.

Before it happened, there were the cases to be argued that would settle the fate of old age insurance and, to a considerable degree, unemployment insurance. On April 26, 1937, with Charlie Wyzanski moving my admission, I became a member of the bar of the Supreme Court of the United States—this because my name was going to be "on the brief" for the United States in both cases. Then I listened with admiring awe to Wyzanski's oral arguments in those cases, delivered without a note.

Finally came the great Monday—Monday was the Court's "decision day"—when the Chief Justice announced the name of the first case to be decided (*Helvering v. Davis*, in which the constitutionality of old age insurance was challenged) and, signaling that the Court's opinion was to be read by its author, nodded to—Justice Cardozo. Victory! My letter of May 25 began: "Dear Ma 'n' Pa—Yesterday was a big day! I hadn't really expected the decision until next week. The result itself was not so surprising, but gratifying nevertheless. Late yesterday afternoon Lois and I went down to see Miss Perkins and split a bottle of (domestic!) champagne with her! Winant called me up, and various telegrams have come in."

Yes, it *was* gratifying, and not too astonishing, because the Court had already upheld the Labor Act, signaling a change in the judicial atmosphere and lineup. But even before that Labor Act decision, while I'd been pessimistic about old age insurance, I had not been worrying about my own future. I had a standing offer of a year's appointment to teach in Harvard's government department. And in late March, I think it was, I had decided to accept that offer.

I didn't particularly want to teach. My ambitions lay elsewhere, and having a job in Cambridge would help me to realize them. They had crystallized at a luncheon meeting, at a Washington hotel, of the Harvard Club of Washington. The speaker was a congressman from Massachusetts—*my* representative, for though I'd spent ten months in Buffalo my legal residence had continued to be the parental home in Cambridge. He was a much-respected, scholarly, elderly Republican, Robert Luce of Waltham. With my own ears I heard him say: "We must not look down upon the poor and the unemployed. It is not their fault. God made them lazy and incompetent."* That evening, on arriving home, I said to Lois: "Better get ready to pack, dear. We're going to run for Congress!"

And that, in Kipling's phrase, is another story.

---

*Mr. Luce apparently liked these sentences; he repeated them, two years later, at a hearing on a housing bill, and thus they made their way into print.

Chapter 7

Forest Reprise

IT HAS NOT been my purpose to write a case study, illustrating how the legislative system works or how a middle-level bureaucrat operates. These might seem to be the subjects of the three preceding chapters. To correct that impression, I return to my opening metaphor: I'm once again a beaver among beavers. As I've said, I don't want to write much about other beavers, even though I'm tempted to do so because some of them were truly remarkable. Quite a few I considered my friends, and some were, indeed, my close friends for the rest of my life or rather their lives, for most of them have predeceased me. I think first of Charlie Wyzanski and Paul Herzog, and then of Jim Rowe; others are Jack Tate, Peter Seitz, Gerry Reilly, and Alexander Hawes. As I write, all but the last two are gone. But I think they'd all agree that any attempt to portray what it was like to be a New Deal beaver would be inadequate if it made only cursory mention of the larger animals in that imaginary forest. If the latter hadn't been present, the former wouldn't have scurried to Washington.

If each beaver—all right, let's call him a young lawyer—were asked to name the three higher-ranking individuals who meant the most to him, there would be a unanimous choice of one person and a great variety of people selected to fill the other two spots. I think all of us, even though few of us met him and very, very few had many significant talks with him, would name Franklin D. Roosevelt. After all, it was *his* New Deal that we were joining. The other two choices would probably depend on which agency the lawyer doing the selecting worked for. Possibly some NRA lawyers would even select General Johnson. Charlie Wyzanski, Gerry Reilly, and I would certainly choose Frances Perkins. And for Jack Tate and me, a sure choice would be John Gilbert Winant. So now I will write about three people, Perkins, Winant, and Roosevelt, hoping that as I do so I can evoke some of the emotions, yearnings, and even laughter that tinctured the life of a young New Dealer.

I'm glad to write about Miss Perkins at this moment. Today's skeptics need reminding that honest, intelligent, dedicated people, with no desire for self-aggrandizement, can accomplish much for the public good through political effort. We have seen how she took the lead in the successful fight for social insurance, but this was only part of her personal ten-point program. When Roosevelt asked her to be Secretary of Labor she presented him with that program, covering not only unemployment and old age insurance, but also, among other things, a minimum wage law, the abolition of child labor, federal conferences to promote state industrial safety laws, and the reorganization of the U.S. Bureau of Labor Statistics. She told the president-elect she'd join his Cabinet if he would support these measures. "Yes, I'll back you," he said, "and I suppose you'll nag me forever about this!" That was in January 1933; six years later the whole program had been accomplished. Yes, indeed, she did "nag," but she did so with a combination of tact, forthrightness, and loyalty that made her persuasive.

When she took the job her handicaps were considerable. She was a woman, something unheard of in a president's Cabinet. She had a fierce sense of privacy that estranged much of the inquisitive press. Her door, as I have mentioned in connection with Senator Harrison, was guarded by that brusque female Cerberus, Frances Jurcovicz. And she was filling a position that the leaders of the American Federation of Labor felt belonged to them. (Their opposition would have been stronger if they had known that the right to organize unions was not on her list

of conditions for taking the job.) Inevitably, too, she forth-
rightly took positions that aroused antagonism and false
charges against her, especially in the wake of the San Francisco
strike in 1934 (about which more shortly).

I was aware of some of these difficulties. I also knew that I
could do nothing about them. Personal loyalty was Miss Perkins's dominating trait, and among the persons she was loyal
to was her secretary, Miss J. It was useless even in the gentlest
manner to criticize Miss J.—even though Pat Harrison was not
the only member of Congress she offended, by any means.

Miss Perkins was truly disappointed when Congress made
the Social Security Board an independent body, outside the
Department of Labor, but she never blamed anyone but herself for that decision. Perhaps she and Miss J., together, were
partly to blame; but actually the decision may have been basically impersonal. The Labor Department had always been
seen, as Miss Perkins's predecessor, William Doak, once told my
father, as the department *for* labor. The senators and representatives with whom I talked frankly in the months when they
were considering the Social Security bill just said that as neither welfare nor old age insurance was an obviously "labor"
matter, an independent agency should handle them.

Still, it must be admitted that her relations with Congress,
and with the press, were never very good and were occasionally
stormy. In March 1935, I was writing unhappily: "My, the Congressmen do dislike Miss Perkins! She had three Ways and
Means members to dinner Tuesday, and tonight one of them
gives the papers a story to the effect that when they see the
President about our bill, they don't want Miss Perkins at the
conference because she'll try to run everything. And the 'journalists' are sore at her because when a photographer exploded
a flashlight in front of her the other day, she reached out and
said 'give me the plate' and tore it up!" And I remember another occasion when, scheduled to testify before a House
committee at ten o'clock, she arrived at eleven, much to the
congressmen's disgust, though she then disarmed them—

somewhat—by answering their questions clearly and knowledgeably.

Charlie Wyzanski and I attended that meeting. We had arrived on time, and had suffered when the committee chairman, Billy Connery, ordinarily friendly to Miss Perkins, called in the newspaper photographers to take pictures of the waiting committee and the empty witness's chair. After she had arrived and testified, and we had sincerely congratulated her, we drove back to the department with her. She said indignantly: "Did you see what Drew Pearson [the most famous Washington columnist of the day] said about me this morning? He called me a bossy schoolmarm. Now, I'm from New England and I know a schoolmarm when I see one and I'm not like that at all! Do *you* think I am?"

We, her courtiers, assured her she was not. Alas, that night we were both guests at a large dinner party at her home, preceding the annual Labor Department dance. All the assistant secretaries and bureau chiefs were there; also, I think, Billy Connery himself. As we were having dessert, Miss Perkins rapped for silence, rose, and addressed us approximately as follows: "This is a really big night for all the stenographers and messengers and other people who are coming to the dance. They've worked hard and they deserve a good time. Now, I'm sure that each of you won't feel it too much of a burden to be responsible for seeing that the employees in your bureau or section or division do all have the wonderful time they're looking forward to. Thank you." She didn't end up by saying, "Thank you, my children," but she might just as well have!

Much more troublesome, to her, than congressional impatience or the Pearson column, was the concerted campaign of vilification that followed the San Francisco strike. This began when I was still in the department and continued until the egregious Martin Dies of Texas, chairman of the House Un-American Activities Committee, sought to have her impeached in 1939. From 1934 on, the slanderous attacks on her had circulated more and more widely: this daughter of a Yankee stationer was really a Russian-born Jew, Matilda Watski; this high-church Anglican was a communist; she—or, sometimes, it was her daughter—was secretly married to Harry Bridges, the radical longshoremen's leader. She bore all this stoically. In April 1936, I went to a very cheerful party at her house where she could still smile scornfully at the gossip about her Russian birth: "Miss Perkins gave a grand dinner—a very stimulating evening. Winant was there, and Secretary Wallace in an unusually jovial mood, and Daisy Harriman and the French Ambassador and the novelist Ernest Poole. Mrs. Poole told awful stories about a 'genealogist' in the pay of the Republican National Committee quizzing Miss Perkins's younger sister and saying 'But you weren't present at the birth of your sister Frances of course. . . .' What dirty business!"

In this context the Secretary did have one triumphant moment, and she told me about it. She went to a conference in San Francisco (soon after the strike) and stayed in a hotel. Late one afternoon she was returning to her hotel room, when she was passed in the corridor by a man in a workman's clothes. Immediately after she had entered her room and shut the door, there was a knock on it. The workman entered, saying, "Aren't you Secretary Perkins?" When she said she was, he continued: "Thought you ought to know: I've just been putting a bug into your room—right there. Hated to do it. Glad I could tell you. Good-bye."

As she told that story, her expression was one of grateful surprise. Seldom, however, did her face reflect either delight or despair. She was that rather unusual combination, a great talker and storyteller and a very private person. Whenever she mentioned her own belief in the importance of privacy, she ascribed it to her New England heritage, but I'm sure it was fostered by the one thing she never wanted to discuss: the plight of her husband, Paul Wilson, who had long been a physical and psychological invalid. He had stayed in New York when she moved to Washington, and was later in a sanitarium in North Carolina; though presumably she kept in touch with him, she could not have seen him often in those busy New Deal years. I don't recall her ever mentioning him.

Nor did I or Charlie Wyzanski ever hear a word from her about religion. Not until George Martin's *Madam Secretary* was published in 1976 did we learn what a large part religion played in her life. We had had no knowledge of her frequent visits to an Anglican convent in Maryland, where she spent much of the time in prayer and the rest in discussing social legislation with the Mother Superior.

A private person, she was by no means a loner. Sharing a house with the very sociable Mary Rumsey (Averell Harriman's sister), she couldn't possibly have been a loner even if she had wanted to. And after Mrs. Rumsey's death in an accident, Miss Perkins kept right on inviting friends to tea or small dinner parties. Several of these I referred to briefly in letters ("met the Irish poet, A.E., at the Secretary's yesterday") and one at some length. This was shortly after my marriage to Lois Jameson. For some reason, Miss Perkins gave a dinner in honor of Emil Ludwig, the distinguished German biographer of, among others, Goethe, Bismarck, and Schliemann. Susannah Wilson, Miss Perkins's teenaged daughter, was present, and so were Lois and I.

> Dinner at Miss Perkins'—highly entertaining. Emil Ludwig was there—a show-off, but amusing. I had the seat opposite him and argued with him considerably. Then Miss Perkins demanded general conversation and answers to his questions. Good but dumb Turner Battle* kept saying "Take Tom: he is serving 120,000,000 people," . . . while the young son and daughter-in-law of sculptor Joe Davidson discoursed on (1) the unpleasantness of being shot at dawn and (2) whether negro taxi-drivers have souls, Mrs. D. being *very* much interested in souls. Susannah Wilson egged her on and poor Miss Perkins got pretty fed up; Ludwig was getting a funny impression of intelligent American youth. Finally Lois got him aside and told him the important news that the Zoo here contained the only known offspring of a brown bear–polar bear union.

*Turner W. Battle, administrative assistant to the Secretary, was an amiable Virginian whom Miss Perkins hoped, unrealistically, would shore up her relationships with Southern politicians.

Seldom, though, was conversation with the Secretary or at her home so frivolous. Unlike some great talkers, she was a good listener too. She and I, usually with one or two others present, talked frankly and freely about the problems confronting the department and the Committee on Economic Security. In these matters she and I realized that, almost always, we saw eye to eye. I remember only one instance in which I was critical of her handling of a difficult issue, and I don't think that I expressed my criticism to her. In March 1935, the Immigration Service caused the arrest of the English socialist John Strachey, apparently because of allegations that he was a communist. "I have been feeling pretty ashamed," I wrote, "about this absurd and indefensible arrest of John Strachey, done over violent protests from this office and without any final commitment from the Secretary." I think that Strachey was released and, facing probable deportation, went back to England without further ado; but the incident was disturbing. It was also rather surprising, for a year or two earlier Miss Perkins had resisted clamorous right-wing protests and admitted the entry of a famous Marxist, Emma Goldman. I think the real mistake, if it was a mistake, was made by the Commissioner of Immigration, Daniel McCormack. He and she were old friends, and her own loyalties extended to her subordinates as well as to her superiors.

It is ironic that the whispering campaign against her focused on her alleged communism, for she was quietly but deeply anticommunist. She wasn't hysterical about it; she wasn't fearful about communism or, I guess, about anything else except invasions of her privacy.

We've seen how she—irritably, to be sure—refused to heed the cries of alarm during the San Francisco strike, and advised the president to reject the frightened pleas for drastic, forceful action. This pattern was repeated in early 1937, when the first major sit-down strike was called by the automobile workers in Detroit. Industrialists and many newspapers demanded violent action to eject the strikers from the factories. There were fears expressed of red revolution—for wasn't the automobile union a branch of the newly formed Congress of Industrial Organizations, and wasn't the C.I.O. a communist organization?* Governor Frank Murphy of Michigan refused to call out the troops; and the pressure shifted to Washington.

Miss Perkins met with the president. They agreed that they didn't *like* sit-down strikes, but "you don't shoot people for trespassing, do you?" Anyway, he wasn't sure that, legally, trespass was involved: she grinned and said to him, "Well, you're a lawyer, aren't you?" As they had in the San Francisco case, they kept their heads and the strike ended without bloodshed.

I was not in the department at the time of the sit-down strikes (though I was in my old office, or rather Wyzanski's, in what had been the Labor Department building; the Social Security Board had taken it over when a monstrous new Labor building was opened on Constitution Avenue.** However, I readily defended the Secretary's action, or lack of action; several letters that winter refer to my rejoinders to criticism of Miss Perkins. More than thirty years later I faced the academic equivalent of the sit-down strike—namely, the campus sit-in. As a university president I heard the demands for violent action—call the police, demand that the governor call out the National Guard, drag the bastards out of there. I refused to act. Like Miss Perkins, I had to shrug off torrents of verbal abuse, and I had the satisfaction of seeing the crisis peacefully resolved.

I can't say that my conduct in the turbulent campus disputes of the sixties was *consciously* modeled on Miss Perkins's in the labor disputes of the thirties, but she probably had influenced my thinking. If so, I am grateful. Indeed, it is with gratitude, more than anything else, that I remember Frances Perkins. That she played a key role in my professional advancement is

*Of course the C.I.O. was *not* a communist organization, but its president, John L. Lewis, had employed Lee Pressman as its counsel. Wyzanski, Reilly, and I had all told Miss Perkins that we assumed that Pressman was a communist when he sought to succeed Wyzanski as Solicitor of the Labor Department. She called Lewis and told him that Pressman would not be welcome at the Labor Department as the C.I.O. representative.

**Today the Labor Department is housed in still another building, fittingly named for Frances Perkins.

obvious. But she was also an understanding, thoughtful friend. Once I wrote home, after spending a feverish weekend in bed, "I went to the office Monday morning and Miss Perkins, knowing I'd been sick, called up to say that my pay would be stopped if I didn't go away." She could and did establish quick and close relationships with young people she deemed promising. I think of Wyzanski, myself, John Steelman briefly, and especially Gerry Reilly. She worked with us as colleagues, never trying to dominate us.

Yes, I recall her with gratitude, and also affection and admiration. She was a good person. She had terrific energy. She knew her stuff: in twenty years of experience in New York she had mastered the whole field of social legislation. She must have been born articulate, and she was honest and fearless. The libelous attacks on her hurt her more than any of her close associates realized, but she weathered them without losing her innate optimism. She remained self-contained and she eschewed self-pity. And finally, she was buoyed up by the conviction that she was doing God's work. George Martin (in his biography) quotes her as saying, "I had to do something about unnecessary hazards to life, unnecessary poverty. It was sort of up to me." The motto of her college class at Mt. Holyoke was "Be ye steadfast." She was.

In the fall of 1935 I was writing to Berresford that I was leaving the Labor Department and was "very lucky to be exchanging one pretty wonderful boss for another that's pretty wonderful, too, in a different way." My new chief was John Gilbert Winant, chairman of the Social Security Board. To describe the impact that he made on me, and to seek the reasons for it, I must break through the time frame of the preceding pages.

I worked for Winant not only from the fall of 1935 to the fall of 1937, but again for seven months in 1943, when he was our ambassador to Great Britain and I was his "special assistant" as well as director of the British Division of the Office of War Information. It was after my return from London, while Winant was still ambassador, that I dropped in to see Jack Tate.

I picked up a copy of the *New York Times* that was lying on his desk. Jack said: "There's a picture on page four. I've got a confession to make." I opened to the page. On it was a picture of Winant. I looked at it silently for several seconds, and then said: "Is your confession the same as mine? Shivers went right down my back when I saw that picture." Jack smiled, nodded, and replied quietly, "Yes, same here!" We were thrilled even by a picture of him.

We were not the only people to be so impressed by Winant, though perhaps not many were so affected by a photograph of him. Yet he did make an astonishing impact. Again in 1943, the annual Lord Mayor's luncheon was held in the shell of the bombed-out Guildhall in London. The British "establishment" turned out in full force, nearly three hundred of them. Winant was to be the speaker. I was seated at the head table across from him—also across from Anthony Eden and Lord Simon. I talked a little with the "press lords"—major newspaper publishers—on either side of me, privately naming them Lords Tololler and Mountararat; and I conversed, too, with Eden and Simon. But not with Winant. He was darkly silent, speaking to no one, scribbling now and then on an envelope he extracted from his pocket. I thought to myself, has all this talk about his being Lincolnian got to him? Does he imagine he's writing the Gettysburg address?

At last the time came for him to speak. He looked unhappily at the notes he had just written; he stared at the audience; then, haltingly, he began his speech. He was audible, though he did not have a ringing voice. He was grammatical, but he had nothing original to say. After every other sentence he paused, for what seemed an eternity, while he thought about what he would say next. "We're in this war together." Long pause. "We're in it together to the end." I was wishing only that his speech would end. He was miserable, I was miserable, the audience must have been miserable.

After about seven minutes of this agony, in the middle of one of those long pauses Winant suddenly sat down. There were several seconds of dead silence. Then—I have never heard anything like it—there was a loud *crash* of cheering, a kind of explosion that lifted everyone to his feet. Lord Mountararat pounded me on the back. Lord Tololler grabbed my hand and shook it, shouting, "Wonderful chap! Wonderful chap!"

However, back at the Social Security Board when he was its chairman, my colleagues and I were not so bedazzled that we became uncritical. I shared Winant's dislike of organization charts. But I was at least mildly upset in the early days when, without asking me, he simply borrowed my best lawyer, Bernice Lotwin, and put her to work answering (for his signature) the great number of letters of congratulation and advice that he was receiving. And he made it harder for me to build a superfine staff because, as I wrote, he "thinks lawyers are fine and likes 'em young, but thinks any salary over $2500 or so is exorbitant."

Upsetting, too, was his attitude toward time; to him, schedules were things to be broken, and appointments were to be ignored when they conflicted with the need, as he perceived it, to spend hours in secluded conference with a particular individual. In other words, he'd have appointments every half hour, from nine o'clock until noon; but the first person he saw had such problems, or interested him so much, that he would spend the entire morning with that person. Not surprisingly, I was writing in late 1936 about the "inaccessibility of Mr. Winant. He works prodigious hours, but doing what, no one knows; and certainly he neglects many things of first importance to any chairman of the Board. But maybe he will get around to them some day."

It was hard, though, to become angry when one was "stood up" in the fashion indicated above. Unlike Miss Perkins, he had a wonderful buffer in his outer office, a charming New Hampshire woman named Mary Healey. She had been his secretary when he was governor of New Hampshire. She understood him and she knew how to mollify the impatient people who were waiting to see him. She knew, and they came to realize, that almost always Winant was waylaid either by someone's constructive ideas that needed to be spelled out in detail, or by his own consuming desire to help an individual who was in serious trouble. For an example of the latter, I again break the time barrier and move ahead to wartime London.

Needing to see the ambassador, I went downstairs to his suite in the embassy and asked the Foreign Service Officer outside his office door, "Is the boss in?" "Yeah," was the gloomy reply. "He's in all right, and you can go in, if you want to enter a bear's den where there's a wounded bear wandering around." I said, "I'll chance it," and opened the office door. The ambassador's office was at least forty feet long, with the desk at the end at which I entered. Winant was pacing at the far end of the room, looking like a thundercloud, or maybe a wounded bear. Then, still silent and tortured, he made a complete circle of the room and began to make another one. When he was about to pass me a second time I stepped forward and asked, "What's the trouble, Governor?" (I usually called him "Governor"; like Senator George Aiken of Vermont, he enjoyed that title.) He looked at me gravely, went to his desk, and picked up a letter. "Oh, God," he said, "I wish Mary were here!" "You mean Mary Healey, Governor?" "Yes. If *only* she were here: she'd know. She'd know." "Know what?" "It's this letter, " he said, "the fellow that wrote it is in great trouble but I can help him. Or, rather, I *could* help him." He looked at me despairingly. "The letter tells the whole story, and then it ends 'Sincerely, Bill.' *Who is Bill?*"

Neither in London nor, earlier, in Washington was Winant an easy person to work for, but I'm thankful that I did not miss the experience. After a luncheon conference that, typically, must have disrupted his schedule for the rest of the day, an October 1935 letter of mine said: "Well, 'Gil' Winant spent three hours with me, or vice versa, yesterday and I guess I have the job. No money so nothing official, but the last doubt seems to have vanished and it can at last be noised abroad that I *am* going to be, or just *am*, General Counsel of the Social Security Board. Winant is a *fine* person, very impressive in a wholly unimpressive way, very slow and very friendly."

Curiously, I omitted from that letter the one thing that Winant said that impressed me most. I did not write about it but I never forgot it. He suddenly asked me, in what I called his "hushified" manner, what single quality was most important for a person in public office to have. Taken aback, I answered, rather tentatively, "Well, integrity I suppose, and intelligence." He shook his head and uttered one word: "Kindness."

His own political gift was his concern for and understanding of individual human reactions. He thought in those terms. A new problem would not be handled necessarily on the basis of objective logic, but on his estimate of how each proposed solution would affect the various people concerned. Some critics called him "no politician," because he never became president and because his support of Franklin Roosevelt made him, a registered Republican, virtually a man without a party. But he was the only man who, up to that time anyway, had ever been governor of New Hampshire three times; he headed both a great federal agency and an important national agency, the International Labor Office, and he was a beloved ambassador. Not a bad career!

Winant combined a conscious religious zeal with political ambition and acumen. Some critics tried to ascribe his acts of Christian charity to his ambition; some admirers saw his political career as his way of serving God. What I perceived was a blended motivation; but what he sought to prove, and proved, was that a man can love mercy and walk humbly and be, withal, a statesman. He proved by example that a man can live his life in politics without losing his ideals and his integrity. His particular qualities—compassion, patience, and a kind of inarticulate fervor for all that is of good report—had a lasting influence on many, many younger people, including me, who were eager to render public service.

If you asked me how my fellow beavers felt about the lion, Franklin D. Roosevelt, I would be tempted to answer in Miss J.'s too frequent words: "I don't know at all. I really can't say."

To all of us he was certainly a presence, whether we saw him or not; in those early years he dominated both the executive and the legislative branches of the government. I assume that some of the young New Deal lawyers felt worshipful and believed that they were ready to follow him anywhere. Some others, undoubtedly, were simply aware of his importance and let it go at that. My own feelings were surprisingly ambivalent.

My first sight of F.D.R. was at the Democratic National Convention in New York in 1924—the convention that was deadlocked through over a hundred ballots and so lost the party whatever chance it had to win the election that November. It was the convention, too, at which Roosevelt, battling polio, made his "happy warrior" speech nominating Alfred E. Smith—a scene made famous by Ralph Bellamy in the film *Sunrise at Campobello.*

I didn't hear that speech. But I came to New York, for I was about to sail for Europe, a real adventure for a seventeen-year-old, and my father got tickets to the gallery at Madison Square Garden. We were there through, I think, the sixtieth to the sixty-third ballot, and I joined heartily in the constant roar of the crowd: "We want Smith!" Between ballots, there was some jurisdictional argument, and Roosevelt, as spokesman for the Smith forces, brought himself forward on the platform and made a few remarks. I was struck then by his good looks, his good voice, and the good sense of what he said.

I was not so impressed, however, that I favored his nomination in 1932. As I have mentioned, I was still sentimentally for Smith. And, as a rather priggish young idealist, I was turned off by Roosevelt's preconvention campaign, which could easily be criticized as being "all things to all men." Another cause for disaffection was the preprimary alliance forged by his son James with the notorious James Michael Curley, the attractive rogue who was portrayed so well in Edwin O'Connor's novel *The Last Hurrah* and the movie of the same name.

However, after F.D.R. (I wonder why I referred to him, in my letters, as "F.D."—I don't recall hearing anyone call him that) was nominated I was able to muster up some enthusiasm, modified by lingering skepticism. The combination is descriptive of my reaction to his inaugural speech on March 4, 1933. Of course I was thrilled by "the only thing we have to fear is fear itself." But later in the speech came a phrase that evoked from me a cynical chuckle: "We must have an adequate but sound currency." A year or so afterwards I was reminded of that phrase when, as I have recounted, I learned that Tugwell had stimulated the president's interest in the Wagner-Lewis bill by his suggestion that the investment of all those vast (nonexistent) unemployment reserves could solve the "currency problem."

It took less than a week after that inauguration to convince me and millions of other Americans that Franklin Roosevelt was the leader the country desperately needed. The economy had hit bottom and was inert; his own brisk confidence enlivened it. He simply assumed the responsibility for reviving it; in effect, he asked the people to trust him and they did. Because they did, Congress did his bidding through the famous first "hundred days" of his administration. By the time I got to Washington those days were over but the glamour lingered: throughout the four-year period that this book covers, he was still dominant, though the voices of opposition were loud and harsh.

The blindly devoted followers of Roosevelt, including, certainly, some of the young lawyers, would take umbrage at those often hateful voices of opposition. I was not among them, as my cheerful acceptance of the Jouett Shouses' frequent hospitality shows, for Jouett Shouse was a real Roosevelt-hater. I was often critical, but quietly so—very critical and very quiet in the matter of the "Court-packing plan," when that preternaturally large and noisy beaver, Tom Corcoran, tried to persuade all of us to rally openly behind the president.

By and large, though, I was a New Dealer and a Roosevelt man. I liked the way he spoke, and came unconsciously (or half-consciously) to imitate him when I myself entered politics;

our articulation and the timbre of our voices were not dissimilar, and early in my first campaign for Congress a newspaper article mentioned my habit of using one of his pet phrases: "You and I know . . ." As an administrator he was often described as unsystematic and inefficient, and many years later when I became a university president I was subjected to similar complaints. This time I was quite aware that I was modeling my administrative style on his, disdaining organization charts, springing surprises, seizing opportunities to please my various constituencies. A university presidency is, after all, very much a political job.

But neither oratory nor executive dexterity made Franklin Roosevelt the lion that he was—already, in Washington, long before he became a great world figure. One of his first and best biographers was Frances Perkins. She stated what made him the great New Dealer: "The New Deal grew out of . . . emergency and necessary rescue actions. The intellectual and spiritual climate was Roosevelt's general attitude that *the people mattered*."* And on a subject dear to her heart and mine, she wrote that "He always regarded the Social Security Act as the cornerstone of his administration and, I think, took greater satisfaction from it than from anything else he achieved on the domestic front."**

So, basically, it is with a combination of admiration and gratitude that I think now of the three remarkable people who so greatly influenced my part of that "forest beside the Potomac" in the four years when I was there. And what was it really like, to be there? The best way to answer that question is to quote Wordsworth:

> Bliss was it in that dawn to be alive,
> And to be young was very Heaven.

---

* Frances Perkins, *The Roosevelt I Knew* (New York: Viking, 1946).
** Ibid.

Index